Teac [illegible] g,
and Learning

Order this book online at www.amazon.com or email orders mary.pound11@yahoo.com

Most Amazon titles are also available at major online book retailers.

Printed in the United States of America.

ISBN: 978-1-7361746-0-9 (pb)
ISBN: 978-1-7361746-1-9 (e)

Library of Congress Control Number: pending

Table of Contents

Table of Contents

What is one of your earliest childhood memories?

This is a memory of Lily's house, and my grandmotherly first babysitter when I was three years old in Seattle, 1954. We were living in West Seattle on 46th Avenue, a few blocks down the street from her house. My mom had recently divorced my real dad, and now she was dating Fritz, my soon to be step father. My mother had to work full time to support herself and her three children. So, I was off to Lily's house each day!

There was a bulldog statue in the hallway leading up the stairs. To me he was a real as a dog could be. He had a stocky little body and was as cold as ice, made of smooth, polished ceramic. But you never would believe what a three year old could imagine about such a dog! He stood about three feet high, but to me he was about my size, but greater and stronger than any real dog could ever be. To me he was solid and strong because he never could be moved, he was stately and kinglike in his formality. We had many great times as I would imagine the ways he would protect me from all the other scary creatures that must have been hiding in all those other rooms upstairs that I wasn't allowed into!

I'll never forget the day I wet my pants and I was so upset with myself because I didn't have any replacements. Lilly took a pair of her silky, absolutely huge panties, and cut them down and scooched up the elastic so they would fit me, and proudly showed them to me like I was supposed to be happy to put them on! I'll never forget the feel of that silk, and I kept on imagining myself in her great big panties all day long!

Her husband, Ed, spoiled me rotten! I'd get there in the mornings before he left for work, and I'd sit princess-like at his knee at the kitchen table. It was homey and they felt like grandma and grandpa and the whole house looked like it was something out of the twenties. I remember distinctly dunking oatmeal iced cookies into milky coffee, and that was our breakfast, as Ed would only eat this each day, and I imagined myself just as grown up as him. I'd dip my cookies into my own cup of coffee, which was mostly whole milk and sugar, and I'll never forget how I knew I was getting away with murder with the both of them! They knew that I knew that they knew too!

I spent the rest of the day in my own imaginary world, fighting off the lions and all the other dangers that were lurking around every corner of that turn of the century house, with my best friend, the ceramic bull dog, who lived in the hallway!

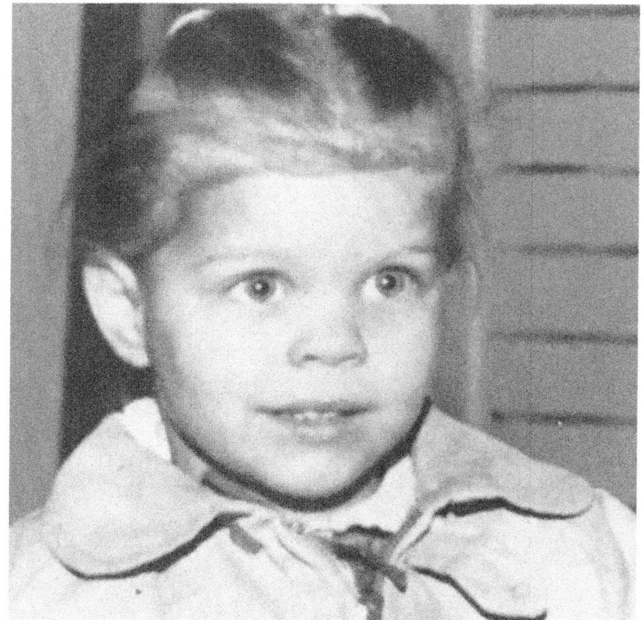

Memories of Aunt Laura's house

Here I am, all of four years old, settling into the slippery back seat of Fritz's red DeSoto, and wind is flying through my hair, and I can taste the sweetness of the wheat kernels on the tip of my tongue just by being in the blustery, summertime air of Eastern Washington. Mom is getting married again and I'm being shuttled off to live with Aunt Laura and her rowdy farm kids for a week, while Mom goes on her honeymoon with Fritz, my new step-dad. My brother Tom doesn't have the time of day for me, and Grant is at a Boy Scout camp for the week, so as soon as Mom drives off I know I best start "making my own way" with the "women folk" I'm left with!

Aunt Laura was the epitome of an old fashioned school teacher - all business, no fuss, no pampering or cuddling or fussing about me. Her husband, Dell, was drinking just about all the time I saw him, when he wasn't out in the fields in his combine harvesting wheat, he was sitting at the kitchen table having another shot of something. Darlene, their only daughter, was in high school trying as hard as she could to look pretty with her turquoise blue Avon jars in the bathroom that I could hardly keep my hands off! I was so intrigued by all her makeups and potions to fancy herself up with. When she wasn't looking, I was sneaking in there to fuss around with them as quiet as a mouse so I wouldn't be discovered!

I knew I was in for trouble the minute I saw Mom and Fritz drive off in a cloud of dust. The entertainment of the week would be Laura's sons, Darryl and David, both farm boy pimply faced fullback looking teenagers, stuck on tormenting me as much as they could! Now mind you, I'm only about four years old and a city slicker and I'm not at all used to farm life! My idea of swimming isn't in a horse trough, but they know they can tell me that's all there is and I'll be hot enough to go in anyway! So there they are - all watching me as I'm practically gagging and throwing up in all that God awful dirty horse water that's probably been in there for ten years! It's a wonder I wasn't sick the whole time I was visiting them! I still remember how gross the water was even to this day.

The other major entertainment included setting me outside their front door, locking it behind them, of course, and letting me just sit there like bait while the biggest, meanest, loudest, ugliest, largest group of honking geese would ramble over to snap at my fingers and toes!! I'll never forget loudly begging to be let in, and those geese tormenting me, knowing how blessed scared I was! I knew if I tried to run away from them I would just be in more dangers, as they would just follow me and I'd be even farther away from safety! Darryl and David would yell through the door and tell me I had to stop crying before they would let me in. I knew being quiet was the only hope for freedom, so I would suck it up and try as hard as I could to shut up. Finally they would relent and let me back in.

But the worst of all was Darryl and David locking me in the meat freezer! They had a walk in freezer the size of a bedroom just off the kitchen! They must have thought it was the funniest sight on Earth to lock their little blond cousin in there and listen to me holler, and see how long they could let me stay in there with all the chunks of meat and packages of vegetables, and what all else! I would cry for a while and then stop crying, thinking that if I was quiet they might open the door to check if I was still alive! Finally, Aunt Laura would discover their devious tactics and insist they let me out! I'd be in there shivering, thinking I was never going to survive that week! I would look at all that dead meat and figure that I was just about a chunk of dead meat myself! They did that a bunch of times, more than I care to remember!

But Darlene was civilized and at least tried to be kind. She fixed up my hair with curlers and bobby pins, and had me all pretty before she took me into town a few times. It was a big deal to see the catalog store for J C Penney's or have an ice cream at the country five and dime.

But what I mostly remember is sitting on that slippery, wooden pew, and looking up at those stained glass windows and the big wooden cross in that little country Catholic Church, and remembering how simple and pure everything seemed, how idyllic and basic life was in the country, and wishing I could be a part of it for some time more. If only they would all stop torturing me!

Here I am at the farm with my mother and a younger cousin, many years later!

The Alligator Story

Memoir of 1955. I was still four years old, and we had moved to a rental house on the North end of Mercer Island, and now my grandmother Emma was living with us, and my two brothers, along with Mom and Fritz.

My mom was working all the time and I remember my grandma watching me a lot, and a whole lot of duck mess was always on the lawn in the front grass down by the dock. I wasn't ever allowed outside by myself because everyone was always afraid I was going to drown. But I do remember looking at all the duck poop and wondering why in the world would anyone think I would want to walk through all that muck to get down to the water anyways?

Well, mom woke up one morning and was sure that I deserved a good hard spanking, and wouldn't you know but she pulled my pants down, and spanked me red handed until I was crying and hollering and begging for mercy!! She'd had a dream that there'd been a slug of alligators down at the lake, and she saw me getting close to them, but as loud as she called to me I wouldn't come to her, and I just kept walking towards those mean ol' alligators! She woke up so darned mad at me, sure that I was going to get eaten up! But then she woke up grateful that she found that it was only a dream. But she said that I must have deserved that spanking anyways because I must not mind her or she wouldn't have dreamed it! So I deserved the spanking for all the times I probably thought about not minding her - even if I did mind!

Go figure that!! That was my mom, and that was only the beginning of my getting the idea that I was dealing with someone who wasn't a normal regular type thinking person... even at four years old I knew had to start being smart as a fox to keep her from getting me like that again!

As I grew older, whenever she thought I deserved a warning or a reprimand, she would say, "Remember those alligators!" as if the whole incident had been real. I would just shrug my shoulders a bit and walk away with a quizzical look on my face, wondering if she really did think it all really happened....but the weirdest part of all is there ain't even been alligators in Lake Washington!!

My First Swimming Lessons at Four Years Old

Fritz was a super salesman, and he had a great reputation as an honest employee who could always be trusted. We all moved to the Chicago suburb of Des Plaines at this time because Fritz took an offer to work as a representative for a company that manufactured heavy duty metal working machines like lathes, drill presses, and other huge machines that companies like Boeing bought to manufacture things like airplanes. He ended up staying at that job for only one year because he missed the Puget Sound and the Seattle waterways so much.

My mom was still always working, so my big brothers Grant and Tom had to have “the Kid”, (me), tail along all the time! And I could tell just by the way they talked to me that they didn’t like this situation very much, or ME! Back then, every kid had to learn how to swim just in case you fell out of a boat or went down to the lake by yourself, so I was no exception. Who else but my brothers got stuck taking me to swimming class?

My brothers would take turns plopping me in the baskets of their big Schwinn rubber tire bikes, and taking off down the busy streets, with my feet practically getting all tangled up in the spokes, and my swimsuit riding up my bottom and my towel wrapped around keeping me from feeling every single bump!

But I still remember thinking it was all pretty great because no one else got to swimming class that way! And besides, I was proud to have two handsome big brothers, even though I didn't think they liked me much! I really don't even remember the swimming part, only the bike rides to and from the pool!

Chasing Fireflies

This memory is another one from Des Plaines, Illinois from probably around 1955-6. You had to wait until it was almost pitch black dark outside, and they mostly only come out in the summertime, and you have to have a jar all ready when they come out! And I remember taking the big, rusty, really sharp ice pick, and jabbing it down with all my might on the lid of that mayonnaise jar, always relieved that one of us didn't get stabbed! I remember thinking someone could really get killed if they used this thing in the wrong way. Nevertheless, we just stabbed away with no supervision and no one took much notice of us, and we would go out back and all around the neighborhood when we were only four and five years old.

The whole neighborhood would be full of kids just like us, chasing those big fiery nighttime bugs! They'd go slow like big fat yellow and black bumblebees, except they had taillights on their behinds, and you could get about twenty or so of them trapped up in your jar. But you had to keep putting the lid back on every time you caught one so they couldn't escape. Then we'd all compare and see who was the best catcher that night, but I think we always let them go right away so that we'd make sure there were enough for the next night! I can't believe the joys of having such a large amount of freedom when I was so little!

Another memory of the Chicago area involved running on the rainy, summer time sidewalks. This happened when we lived in an inner city Chicago urban area for a while before we moved to Des Plaines. Now I was really only four years old. We lived in a two or three story larger type house, with a lot of other similar style homes on our block. We all had back yards fenced in where we could play too. Our back yard had lots of garter snakes, and I would play with them for hours thinking they were my personal friends.

On super rainy, steamy hot summer Chicago days we would get in our swimsuits as soon as we saw the rain clouds gathering, and then when the downpour started we would all swing back our front doors and race as fast as we could out to the sidewalk that encircled our neighborhood! And would run as fast as we could, the rain streaming down our slick little bodies and no shoes on and just wild as the wind. All the kids were giddy with delight, and then when we got tired or the rain stopped , we'd all go back into our homes and quietly get back to paying our solitary games again! I never had any memories of playing with those kids, or visiting any of their houses, or even getting to know their names! I only remember just running around the block in the rain with them!

Mom's Surprise

One of my very fondest childhood memories at age four happened in Des Plaines, outside of Chicago. My mom worked as a bookkeeper in a lumber company. I'll never forget one day she told me she had a great big surprise, and came and picked me up at the babysitter's, and took me back to work with her. It was late afternoon, and I remember so clearly what a very big special occasion it was. We bounded out of the car and I remember so clearly walking and "whispering quietly" across the crunchy, brown grasses with my mom. Little did I know then how many more times in my life we would be sneaking around together in our lives! That's a whole "nuther" story!

We finally came upon a hole in the side of the company, right by where the wood building frame and the dirt meet. She whispered to be quiet, and wouldn't you know right there in front of my eyes were the cutest, cuddliest, most adorable, baby brown snowshoe bunnies you had ever seen in your whole entire life?

I remember looking up doe-like into my mother's eyes and squeezing her hand so tightly, and I'll never forget how soft her hands were, they always felt just like velvet. And thinking she was the most absolutely, most wonderful, most marvelous, most beautiful, most caring mom in the whole wide world! And how happy I was to be lucky enough to be her last born little daughter. My mom always had a way of being a surprise to me. She never was predictable. You really couldn't count on her, but she was always one to have something tucked up her sleeve that would come jumping out and provide the best kind of fun. No one else could think of fun the way Mom could. She was zany, wild, unpredictable, impetuous, vivacious, fun-loving like no one else I've ever known.

The other side to her was to come roaring out later - but right now she was most most wonderful mom, and I looked up to admiringly.

What was your Mom like when you were a child?

My mom could best be described as a "real kick"! She was silly, unpredictable, and a real individual. She had a zany personality which could almost be scary at times. She obviously had a lot on her plate as a single mom with three kids before she married Fritz. She must have started dating him when I was just 1 -1/2 years old, because I have seen pictures of the five of us in a small fishing boat in Puget Sound, when I was just crawling to touch the fish that we would catch. Grant and Tom looked to be about 12 and 9 when these photos were taken.

Fritz was my "rock", whereas Jerry was the one whose decisions about my life affected me the most. Jerry had to work full time when I was young, so I had a series of babysitters. Consequently, my brothers took on a lot of the responsibility of watching over me, and making sure I was where I was supposed to be. I think they grew to resent this quite a bit.

Jerry raised me to be very independent. We finally moved back to Seattle during the summer after my kindergarten year. Fritz didn't care how much he was paid, and even would take a pay cut if he could be back to his beloved Puget Sound and the wonderful water ways of the Seattle area.

I remember walking seven or eight blocks to first grade with my little school friends in West Seattle. I had a house key around my neck to let myself in. I also was able to take city busses to downtown Seattle to check myself into he dentist and get back to school safely at the age of 7. By the age of 8, I took multiple busses with transfer passes to get to Brownie camp on the other side of Seattle by myself. I also got myself to Catechism classes at the Catholic Church in West Seattle on Saturday mornings. Pretty independent for a little blondie, don't you think? Jerry never seemed to wonder if I had any troubles on any of these trips. She had all kinds of confidence that I would figure out how to be okay, I guess. Here I am in the middle, with the long blonde hair and short bangs with all my little first grade buddies in West Seattle, and my mom.

As I grew older, and we moved to Mercer Island, Jerry started to exhibit more signs of instability. These episodes caused me to question her sanity and mental health, but in those days in age we never would have said anything. We lived in a time when families kept their family business to themselves. I never would have even talked to Fritz about my worries about her. It just wasn't okay to question anything about your elders. This quiet strength I had to develop at a young age taught me to be even more strong in my dependence upon myself, which may or may not be a good thing! Even to this day, I find myself getting strength more from quiet contemplation and prayer than from asking for help from others. It all started when I was a child. Here I am in my Second grade in my Brownie uniform.

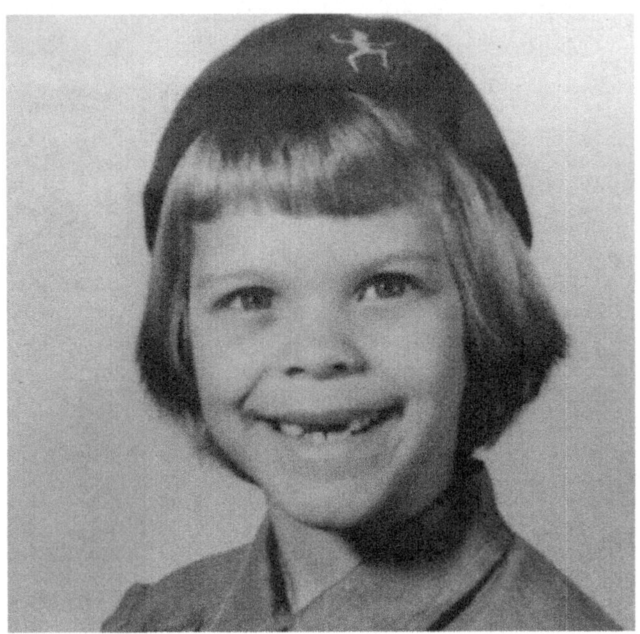

What were your favorite toys as a child?

I have the weirdest memories of my "toys". They weren't really stuff you would play with. They always had to do with making something. My first memory that popped into my brain was my Rosemary Clooney paper doll set. I would spend hours cutting out the figures and clothes, and fantasizing about what it would be like to be such a fancy lady. I remember making sure I cut them out right on the lines to not mess them up.

My next memory had to do with being a little bit naughty. I remember Christmas shopping with my mom and dad at a really big toy store when I was about nine. I fixated on a bank that was shaped like a dog, and somehow the money went in where his tongue was, or something totally strange like that. I wanted that bank more than anything else in the entire store. I pretended to be asleep in the car on the way home, and I overheard them talking about how they had purchased that bank for me. I remember smugly smiling out of their sight, and feeling very satisfied but very secretive at the same time!

All my other memories had to do with making stuff. I started knitting when I was seven or so, and took a sewing class at nine. I actually machine sewed a sailor dress with a mitered collar at nine! I embraced my Girl Scout handbook like it was a Bible and started earning badges around ten. Almost every day I was working towards some sort of badge, like backyard camping, or baking cookies, or wood building. When I was about twelve I remember Barbie L. and I used 2 by 4s to make stilts and would walk around the neighborhood on them, dragging them around to each other's

houses. We also made forts in the woods around the South end of Mercer Island, and were always creating stuff for our pretend camps. Obviously, I was alive when the first Barbie dolls came out and I insisted to have a blonde "bubble" haircut on mine so I could pretend it was me. Here I am, with our favorite neighbor's dog, Rexie, at about age seven.

What was your Dad like when you were a child?

I had two dads. My birth father's name was Raymond Rowe and I barely knew him. According to stories I have heard, he and my mother married rather late for people in that day and age. He was a high school history teacher in his late thirties when he and my mom married. People always said he was a charismatic, dapper, handsome charmer who swept my mother off her feet. My mother was quite a bit younger, just out of college. They had two sons together, and then I came along when Grant was ten and Tom was seven. About this time, they were having lots of marital issues, and he lost his job at the high school, because he was drinking on the job, and he became my babysitter. Probably not a great time to be born!!

I have no memories except one, and it is very sad so I better warn you. My mother found out the hotel or boarding house he was living in somewhere in downtown Seattle. So on Father's Day, when I was seven years old, she had the idea that the three kids could go visit him and surprise him. We knocked on the door,

and he refused to come out to see us and was yelling at us to go away!! I know this is a very sad only memory of my real father. Then about two years later, when I was about nine we received a phone call on Mercer Island that he had passed away. I remember feeling weird and relieved and kind of empty when I heard this news. I have no memories of Grant or Tom's reaction to this very sad news.

Now for a totally different kind of story!! My step-dad Fritz was such a great and positive influence in my life. I think he influenced my future development in more ways than I could even imagine! So many wonderful, loving memories from the earliest times. I remember fishing in Puget Sound and crawling down the boat to touch each fish! Camping trips with trout fishing adventures, and cabin cruiser rides through the locks out through the Deschutes Canal and all around the Puget Sound,

and many, many memories of him holding me on his lap and loving me so much! Getting up on weekend mornings and singing hymns in the kitchen as he made us pancakes and waffles and other yummy treats. He always told me that "being a lady" was the most important thing to accomplish, and that my reputation was what I always had to preserve. He would "ground" me for the slightest infractions, like leaving a wet towel on my bedroom floor, just to keep me from attending boy/girl parties that he didn't approve of.

I always had a list of chores I had to accomplish before he got home from work, and I would recruit my friends to do weird tasks like pulling horsetail weeds down the driveway so that I could play with them again the next day! Fritz was the most honest, full of character, kindest, most respectable, hardest working, and most loving person in my life. He truly influenced me in ways I cannot fathom. He was a true gift from God to me.

More memories of West Seattle

Well, you see back then when we were just six years old and first graders, we used to just walk about the ten blocks to school all in a clump of kids, and nobody even even thought we wouldn't be safe getting there! The old man, Mr. Smith, next door was really scary, but we just didn't look in the windows at him, even though those peaches on his trees looked awfully tempting. We always just looked straight ahead until we got past his house.

I remember Carol and Elaine were my best friends and Steven Hanson lived on the corner, and I told my mom I was going to marry him someday because he was rich and he had a swimming pool, and besides his last name was Handsome and who wouldn't want to be married to someone like that? My mother was rather surprised to find out that what I meant by a swimming pool was one of those four feet in diameter blow up plastic jobs! But we all loved Steven Handsome no matter how big his pool was!

I remember counting the cracks in the sidewalks and meandering on our way down the path in no hurry. But I never remember being late to class, but don't ask me because it seemed like getting to school was the last thing on our minds! The playground was big and had a chain link fence, and there was a movie theatre right around the corner from school where we could go to the movies on Saturdays for a quarter, and we'd just walk there by ourselves. We hardly ever had parents watching over us, except at Brownie meetings where we'd be glueing those macaroni letters on the wooden plaques for some Mother's Day present or something.

At lunchtime we were kind of a little gang, and when we'd feel like it we would walk over to the tiny little Ma and Pa corner store a few blocks from school, and spend our lunch money on frozen candy bars or ice cream bars. I always remember I better eat them carefully in case I chipped my tooth on that frozen candy bar, and then I'd get caught! But that never kept us from sneaking out! That store owner never once said anything to us or the school or our parents! It was our own secret, and he just let us have it!

But the best memory of first grade was taking dance classes for ballet and tap at Hiawatha Park across the street from the school. I would carry my dance gear with me to school, and walk by myself across the park to go to my classes a couple times a week, when I didn't have Brownie meeting. We probably had forty kids in the classes in a great big gym with slippery, shiny wooden floors. I wanted so badly to be noticed for my dancing skills! We were going to have a performance for all the parents, and you better believe I wanted to be in the front! So when they explained that we were going to do a Bunny dance, and we would be wearing pink, stretchy leotards with bunny ears and tails, I set my mind to making sure I was on my very best behavior and super attentive to the lessons so that I could be the leader of all the bunnies in a line! And guess what? My plan worked! I did get picked to lead all the other bunnies around the entire dance floor! I still have that little pink leotard, so that I will never forget how special that day was! I felt like I was the only one on stage and so proud to be the front bunny! It taught me if I really tried and set my mind to something I could succeed!

Growing up Catholic

This memory starts when I was nearing age seven and taking the bus to get to Catechism class at Holy Rosary Catholic Church in West Seattle. You had to take lessons from real nuns wearing black long gowns and those starchy white headbands, and no makeup, and no hair showing, in order to pass the requirements to go to your First Communion. Most little kids took this at age seven. I guess they scheduled these classes mostly on Saturday mornings because parents worked, and kids back in those days had their weekends pretty much free. We didn't have the whole litany of soccer teams, and gymnastics lessons, and the whole other bunch of kinds of activities that keep families busy on Saturday mornings back then.

I would get on a city bus and get myself there in time to go into the donut store on the corner by the church and buy myself a chocolate raised donut before class. That was my prize for making it there on time and safely by myself. Besides, no one was there to tell me I couldn't have one!

The nuns were strict and very somber, rarely acting friendly or welcoming to us kids. They strictly educated us in the Catholic dogma, and made us recite back multiple times the prayer of confession, the Our Father, and the Hail Mary. We were scared to speak, and when asked to answer a question we would all "quake in our boots" and barely get the words out! These classes went on for months and months to finally prepare us for our First Communion ceremony in the springtime.

After class was over, what do you think I did again? Went straight back to that donut store and got another one! Back on the bus, full of sugary goop, and walked back home again. All alone, as I was the only little Catholic on my street.

Buying the First Communion dress, gloves, socks, veil, and shoes, and a special prayer book with an angelic looking praying child on the front was a huge big deal. We all had to dress up like little angels, looking pure as the white driven snow, while we filed up solemnly to stick out our tongues in front of the priest, while we kneeled to receive our First Holy Eucharist. This whole act was freaky scary too.

But before Holy Communion, on Saturdays we had to go to the confessional booth during confession hours and tell the priest everything we did wrong that week, and then go out into the pew again and pray our prayers of penance. Depending on how many sins we had committed, the longer we had to pray prayers of forgiveness. I figured that I had probably done more sinning than all the other little kids, and besides, the priest would like me better if I had to pray a longer time to ask for my forgiveness, so I got in the habit of making up a bunch of sins just so I could really get clean! Some of my most frequent confessions including hitting my brothers, lying to my mother, disobeying my Father, thinking bad thoughts about my friends, and not listening very well to my teachers.

Eventually, I went on to live on Mercer Island and attended St. Monica's Catholic Church. My mother would occasionally attend with me, but she was not allowed to take Holy Communion, because she said that it was against the rules because she was unclean due to her divorcing my dad Ray, and therefore she was excommunicated by the Catholic Church forever. I don't know if they have changed the rules nowadays, and I think they probably have, but anyway, Mom would sit and watch me as I went up alone to get my communion wafer. It always stuck to the roof of my mouth, and I always felt guilty as I tried to pry it off with my tongue, thinking I was hurting the Lord Jesus as I did!

Then the classes for Confirmation started up! We still had to go through a whole stretch of months and months of classes, learning more about church history and all the saints, and finally we were told we must pick a new name for ourselves for our Confirmation. I picked Mary Theresa because I liked the sound of it, and I remember the name had something to do with a pretty flower.

After I became fourteen or so, and started going to dances at the nearby Protestant Churches with all my teenage friends, I started to drift away from the Catholic Church. I no longer pressured my mother to take me to Mass on Sundays. Some of my friends were going to these meetings on Wednesday nights called New Life, and I remember wondering what was different about those meetings from what I knew, but I never had the courage to ask anyone to take me to one. I pretty much dropped off of going to church until I started getting curious again about the age of 18 when I went off to college in Pullman.

Every once in a while I think back and remember how devout I was as a little girl, kneeling at my bedside with my little prayer books. I still have the original one I had at my first communion in a drawer in my house right now! And occasionally I go to the St Justin's Catholic Church in my neighborhood and remember fondly my days attending my childhood Catholic churches.

What were your grandparents like?

I actually have very few memories of interactions with my grandparents. Most of them had already passed away by the time I was born. I do, however, have stories I can recall that had been shared with me about their lives and personalities.

My Grandfather Dave Grant was an engineer on the railroad in Central and Eastern Washington. My mother told me that he was a jovial, fun-loving, and sometimes unpredictable Irish gentleman, who would occasionally have to do weird acts of kindness to regain his good graces with his wife. She told me that he would stop the train and get out and pick wild flowers and watercress on the side of the track to bring back to her to sweeten up her mood! The people on the train got used to it, and they would chuckle to themselves and probably think that old Dave must have been up to trouble again, and needed to sweeten up Emma! My mom said he was fun and laughed a lot.

His wife, Emma, was a more stern German woman who didn't always appreciate his rather wild side. She enjoyed taking my mother to get her hair done and clothes shopping. My mother went on to be an Apple Blossom princess her last year of high school, traveling around the state with the other royalty, and receiving her lessons on the go. I wonder if her beauty was accentuated by all those trips to the beauty salons! This grandmother lived with us for a while when we lived in the rental house on the lake on the north shore of Mercer Island when I was four years old. But unfortunately, I have no memories of her. She apparently had breast cancer and passed away before I could get to know her.

My real dad, Raymond Rowe, was raised in Northport, Washington. He and his father were clearing land and had to blow up some stumps with dynamite. His father lit the fuse and waited and waited and it did not blow up. Finally, he went to check it and my dad watched his own father die when the dynamite exploded just as he was near! His mother was left alone to raise her four children by taking in laundry. I never met them. What sad lives!! Here I am with my maternal grandmother, Emma, at about one year old.

Did you have any serious incidents as a child?

This is a story of two of the naughtiest things I did as a child!! One summer, I think I was about seven years old, my mother thought it would be best if Aunt Elsie babysat me at her home in Seattle. I did not have any friends in that neighborhood, nor did she know any of the kids who lived around her. She would feed me peaches with toast every morning with milky tea. Then we would work out in her backyard and front gardens taking care of her chrysanthemum bushes and tulip beds. She would then do a little housework and I was left free to roam around her house, centering mostly on pretending I was a fancy lady in her bedroom, trying on little bits of her perfumes and creams. There was no television or radio that I ever knew of in her home. Nor any toys or games or puzzles. It was basically the most boring summer you could imagine!

Every once in a while I would convince her to let me walk to the local grocery store, about four blocks away, by myself, to buy a few comic books or coloring pads or something. Some days I would gaze longingly at the boy and girl who lived across the street, making them very aware that I was watching as they put their pool toys or bikes into their mother's car, as they were about to go off on some fun journey. I wanted so much to be invited too! But it never happened.

Well, one day I was so bored I decided I would shake things up a bit. I crawled up the attic at the top of her house while she wasn't looking, and pretended to fall asleep. I eventually heard her yelling my name and calling for me. But I would not answer! That was when things got a little bit crazy. I heard her calling the neighbors over to help look for me. Soon the fire department showed up and they tore the house and neighborhood apart searching for me. All the while I was pretending to be asleep! A fireman found me in the attic, and of course I never fessed up to the mischief I had caused. Guess what? That night Aunt Elsie must have had a big talk with Fritz and Jerry, and I never had to go back to her house to have her babysit me again.

The other really naughty act I did was when I was about nine years old on Mercer Island. I was the new kid on the block, and lots of the neighbor kids had stay- at- home moms who would teach us various things like sewing and knitting. Of course, my mother worked and didn't supervise me after school. So I was free to roam around the neighborhood and the woods nearby our house any time I wanted to. I got the bright idea one day to make a little fort in the woods behind the bus stop at the top of the hill. They were starting to build new homes back there, but it was a relatively secluded spot. I got the idea that we could take some of the candles from the dresser drawers in my mom's storage room, and we could pretend we were pioneers and make a little fire at our camp. It was all well and good, nobody ever let a fire get out of hand or anything, and luckily I was able to contain and control the fires well enough and put them out sufficiently that there never was an incident. But when the neighbor learned from his daughters that we were doing this he was furious and had a big honcho meeting with all the parents involved!! I was the instigator-agitator in the incident, and I was grounded from playing with their kids for a great big long time!!! Eventually, the father sort of forgave me, but I never really felt welcome at their house after that. I learned a big lesson about being sneaky again!!

What was the neighborhood you grew up in like?

West Seattle was my first real home. I lived there until I was eight, except for a few years when we lived in a rental house on the North end of Mercer Island, and the one year we lived in Chicago. West Seattle was a typical neighborhood of one family residences, except for a few taller boarding house residences. My baby sitter, Lily, lived a block away with her husband. She lived in a taller, old style home with winding staircases and scary upstairs bedrooms. I have so many memories of eating cookies for breakfast, and having imaginary friends in the nooks and corners of her house. I think I was the only little child she took care of, I never remember any other kids there with me.

It was in the early 50's, when kids just roamed around the neighborhood, riding our bikes and knocking on each other's doors to ask if any one wanted to play. We pretty much took care of ourselves, playing in the streets, sidewalks, and alleys, with the whole run of the neighborhood. We had a scary old man next door who was a recluse who never talked to us, and we were always running away if we saw him. If we wanted to really be adventurous, we could walk all the way down to Alki Beach on a wooded trail. I only remember doing that once. The best part of Alki beach was Spud's Fish and Chips. We'd soak the fish in vinegar and eat the salty fries with gobs of ketchup until we were stuffed full.

We moved to Mercer Island on Avalon Drive when I was at the end of Third grade. Tarywood Brownie Camp just happened to be located on the south part of the island. The actual camp where we slept and had most of our activities was in the middle of a forest right about 3 miles from our new home. I attended that camp between Third and Fourth grades, and I thought it was so cool that I lived so close that when we hiked down to the lake to go swimming my mom and dad could drive by in their speedboat and wave to us!

Living on Mercer Island as a kid was like heaven on earth. We could ride our bikes, hike through the woods to the store to buy candy, make forts in the woods, swim in the lake, row our dingy row boats to each other's houses, trick or treat around the lake streets with no supervision, and best of all, sled down the big hills on each end of our street on the snow days. We took the school bus to school, and had to hustle up the steep hill every morning to get to the bus on time. We had to wear boots if the day was rainy, and we had to wear dresses or skirts to school every day. If it was a snowy day, school would usually be cancelled, and we'd spend the day sledding down the hills. It was a very big deal if we got to wear pants under our dresses on very cold days.

When I was in about Seventh grade, my friend Ricky P. had horses that we could ride after school. We would each "adopt" one of her horses, and it would become ours. He dad worked as a defense attorney in Seattle, and lots of times his clients were so broke they would pay him in things like horses instead of money. We would ride throughout the wooded trails all over the island, never telling our parents where we were going or what time we would be back. Talk about freedom!! It was seriously the best.

On the weekends, we would have over nights at each others houses, and lots of times my friends and I would sleep outside on the lawn in front of my house. We'd sometimes wake up to slug tracks all over our sleeping bags in the mornings! When we were in about Eighth grade, we would sneak up to the bus stop and meet up with the boys who had spent the night at Sam L.'s house. We would just meet up, say hi, and race back home!

In the summertime we had swim team practice in the lake at the Mercer Island Swim Club, which was right on my street. Sometimes we would get to practice early and dare each other to swim bare naked before the rest of the team showed up! The mornings on Lake Washington were foggy and overcast almost every morning when we had to swim. We just didn't think much about it and just dove right in. Eventually we got a real swimming pool for the swim team, but by that time I was already in high school and too interested in boys to be swimming on the team anymore. Cheerleading took over my interests by then! The first picture is on the grass in my front yard with all my swim team friends. The second one is the photo that appeared in the Mercer Island Reporter when we became cheerleaders in Junior High School.

SMJH CHEERLEADERS

Mrs. Brown

This story happened fourth grade at Lakeridge Elementary School on the south end of Mercer Island. It must have been in about 1960. I remember it was the year of the election between John Kennedy and Richard Nixon. My dad Fritz was a huge supporter of Nixon, and my mom was a Catholic, so she thought it would be great if we had a Catholic president, so she supported Kennedy. I had no idea what the difference was between the two, but the school bus driver thought it would be fun to have the kids sit on the sides of the bus that showed how their parents were voting on the day of the election. He told us when we got on we either had to pick a side, and wouldn't you know most of the kids were jammed in, all squished up, sitting on the Nixon side! Mercer Island was a rather affluent area and apparently most of the parents leaned more towards the Republican side of things. I went ahead and plopped down on the Kennedy side, probably just be be different than most of the others.

Anyway, my teacher was Mrs. Brown that year. She looked like she was near retirement age, had tightly curled grey hair that was colored with a purple rinse, and she was strict and you better not cross her! Of course, this was my first year going to that school, and I was probably more chatty than I needed to be. We had a full class of over thirty students, no aides in the classroom to help her, and little or no support from parents or any one else. She ran a very tight ship, and I was probably "jicky" and wiggly, and already getting interested in boys!

It was Thanksgiving time, and we had a great delicious lunch in the cafeteria that day, slices of juicy turkey, mashed potatoes with gravy, rolls with butter, corn and peas, and pumpkin pie! I ate every last bit on my tray, and when I came back into the classroom my tummy started grumbling and I was feeling overly full. Without meaning to, my tummy just exploded inside and I ending up releasing a loud belch, which I am sure was loud enough for the entire class to hear! The kids, of course, started laughing, and Mrs. Brown scowled and immediately asked, "Who did that?" All the kids turned around and pointed at you know who!! She took me by the arm and led me out of the classroom and scolded me and told me to sit right there!

Our school was built with a long indoor hallway, with coat racks and places to put our boots and umbrellas, and all of a sudden I heard the footsteps of the principal approaching the door at the end of the hallway. I was so scared of him that I hid amongst all the coats, and tried to the best of my ability to disappear! It must have worked because he just walked on past. In those days, if kids were bad, we all heard stories of the boiler room where the principal would take the naughty kids for a whipping with a ruler or big plank of wood. I sure didn't want that!!

Eventually, Mrs. Brown came out of the classroom and was calling my name and looking for me down the hallway, looking even madder than she was before. I got my courage up to peek my little head out from amongst the coats and boots and told her I was sorry, that I really didn't mean to do that. She let me back in, as I held my head down in shame and reentered the classroom with all my friends again! I know you find it hard to believe, but I never did have to visit the principal's office all throughout my education, even in junior high and high school!

More Mercer Island childhood memories

We lived at the South end of Mercer Island, and we had pretty much everything a kid could ever want as our choices. I had to take the bus to and from school everyday and Mom and Fritz worked in the Industrial part of Seattle at Sistig Machinery and Equipment Company, a company my dad started all by himself. He sold heavy duty machines and equipment companies like Boing used to build great big stuff like airplanes. He was a super salesman, and people knew that if he gave his word on something he sold you, and if anything went wrong, he was honest and would make sure you got taken care of.

Over the years he built it up to be a very successful, very lucrative business, with my mother as his head bookkeeper and bill collector. I would spend many weekends in our dining room at home in the beginning years of his company gluing labels on newspapers that he would send out to all his customers.

Because nobody was at the house all day, Fritz got the idea that he would need a watch dog to look over the place and bark and scare away any strangers. Plus, the dog could protect me when I got home from school by myself each afternoon. He decided on a brown Labrador hunting dog we named Rusty. The only problem was that Rusty was such a good watch dog he would bark like crazy at me too when I came home! I was scared to death he was going to bite me, so I had to come up with an ingenious way to make him my friend. I wrote a little note and pasted it on the front inside flap of our mailbox which was located at the top of our driveway, explaining to the mailman that I was going to keep a small plastic bag of dog biscuits in there each day to feed to my grouchy dog as I came home. My system worked perfectly. When I say Rusty bouncing up the driveway to defend his property and chase me off, I would quickly open my bag and throw the group of dog biscuits at him, and he would get so busy eating he would forget to bite me. I don't know how long it took for Rusty to like me, but I do remember most of the time we had him I was scared of him!

Every once in a while Jerry would get the idea that she needed help taking care of all the housework and would stay home a morning once a week to have a cleaning lady come from the inner city of Seattle to help her. All these cleaning ladies were Black and came mostly from the neighborhood right off the

Floating Bridge by Garfield High School. Back then Seattle was pretty much divided into racial neighborhoods. There were the Black area, the Japanese area, the Chinese area, and the Filipino areas. I know calling them "cleaning ladies" is not politically correct these days, but that is what my mother called her.

These women would take the city bus that came all around the island a couple times a morning, and a couple times in the afternoon to take them to and fro back to their neighborhoods in the inner city of Seattle. They would bring big empty plastic tote bags with them each morning, with the hopes that the rich white women would send them home with discarded old clothes, household goods, food, and other things that they might have ordinarily given to the Goodwill. The cleaning ladies would trudge back up the hill to the bus in the afternoon, their tote bags bulging full of all the stuff, and take it back home for their families and friends. It was a very efficient system!

This is where my story gets really interesting. Mom was starting to have many signs of some mental illness about this time, and was quite often acting paranoid that people were spying on her, taking things from her that didn't belong to them, and generally being suspicious quite a bit. We had to listen to her complain about Fritz's daughters and their husbands, various neighbors, and Fritz's work associates quite a bit. We pretty much had the same cleaning lady each week, and Jerry was generous with her, always giving her meat on her sandwich at lunchtime because she knew she would like it. She would pile her up with clothes and other things she wanted to get rid of just like all the other employers. But one day, Jerry got the idea that her cleaning lady was stealing from her, and tucking things in the bottom of her tote bags that she had no right to!

Jerry dressed up in a disguise of a wig and sunglasses and weird clothes, put me in the back seat of her car, and drove to the house where she figured the cleaning lady lived. She was going to sneak into her backyard and look in her windows and see for herself if she could find some of the stuff she took without permission! Now mind you, I'm about nine years old, old enough to know that this is not normal, and highly dangerous. You should have seen how run down the neighborhood was where she was sneaking about! I ducked down as far to the bottom of the back seat of the car as I could go, and hid and prayed for dear life while she snuck around! She came back empty handed, and no one saw her as far as I knew. It was one of the freakiest things I had ever seen!

About this time, many new houses and gardens were being built on the other side of Avalon Drive, not on the waterfront side, but on the facing the street side. Mom got the idea that when she came home from work, she would see pockets of bare earth where she could have sworn there had been a full plant there the day before. Then she would see that these were the same kinds of plants that were being freshly planted in the gardens across the street by the landscapers. Jerry was sure that some of these plants had been taken from her yard. So in the dark of the night she would go up to these freshly planted new yards and dig up the plants to take home and put back where she thought they had been taken! Fritz and I tried as hard as we could to convince her that this was not good, and eventually she stopped. Thank God I don't think anyone in the neighborhood knew that she had been the thief! I was only nine at the time, and I sure do remember thinking that I had better get ready for lot of other adventures ahead with my mother. The photo above is with Fritz and Rusty, the mean dog, when I was about thirteen. The photo below is one of the few of all of us, all dressed up, when I was about nine.

My Brothers and I

You see, my mother and I are really an awful lot alike. She didn't want to be pregnant anymore, so when I was about to be born she decided to throw a big, energetic party for my brother Tom at Alki Beach. She was out running in the sand with all the other seven year old boys with sand in her shorts and barefoot and playing volleyball and ended up going into labor with me during the party! Now how do you think my seven year old brother Tom felt about having a baby sister born on his own birthday?

Obviously he wasn't thrilled when his party was cut short, and he woke up to find out the next day that he would be sharing his birthday with me the rest of his life. I feel like he never let me forget that it was his birthday first, and not mine!

Back when we lived in Seattle and Mercer Island, there were a lot of rainy days and the fashion of the day was old-fashioned rubber boots, the kind you wore over your shoes. Of course, the only shoes that were acceptable for school were oxfords, saddle soap oxfords made of real leather. Ours were a creamy beige color that we proudly wore with corduroy jumpers and heavily starched ironed blouses. I remember fondly covering up my saddle shoe oxfords with leather soap and rubbing them with waterproof greases until they glistened. But still this wasn't enough for my parents! They were concerned that I would fall ill, or they might have to prematurely buy more shoes for me if I didn't go through the additional task each day of buckling my rubber boots over my shoes to wear to school each rainy day. You see, I had to walk quite a distance to the bus stop at the tippy top of a steep hill, and everybody knows that water runs down hills, and does not stay on the flat ground. So, I would like a sweet obedient daughter set off each day in my boots. But, as soon as I got to the bus stop I'd hide them in the bushes behind the enclosure, and set off happily on my way to school, free from those darn old boots! I accomplished being a fashion statement for all my school friends, and my parents never did discover my disobedience! My brothers never knew either.

When my big brother Grant went off to college in Pullman, Washington, I remember baking him endless packages of cookies. And I also recall that many times they had burnt bottoms! But he said he appreciated them, and would write back letters to me and call to let me know I should keep sending them!

It just so happened that one of my big brothers was in charge of taking care of me in the summers when we first lived on the south end of Mercer Island on Avalon Drive. He controlled my behavior in two very strange ways. One, if I had to take a bath he made me sing the entire time I was in the tub. If I stopped singing, he would yell at me to start up once again. I imagine this was his way of making sure I had not drowned in the bathtub.

Secondly, my brother figured out all kinds of devious means to keep me from going near the water. He assigned me endless chores to do including ironing shirts, baking, and cleaning tasks. But the most ingenious method to keep me away from the lakefront had to do with my boots! At the beginning of a hot summer day, I distinctly remember my brother Tom explaining to me in a firm and every serious tone how imperative it was that I wear the boots when I wasn't in the same room with them. His logic was if I had my tight fitting boots on, I would surely know that I had to stay away from the water because everyone knows that boots fill up with water and when they are full you sink! So surely if I had my boots on, the problem was eliminated! The really ridiculous part was I actually believed that my boots were keeping me safe! I was scared to death to even go near the dock if I had them on, so that summer I was kept from drowning once again thanks to Tom's ridiculous trickster tactics! My brothers really did have amazing control over me! The picture below is of my brothers, and my cousins from Spokane, on a hunting trip with our beloved Fritz.

Where did you go on vacations as a child?

My first memory of a "vacation" was visiting my Aunt Laura and Uncle Dell's wheat ranch in Central Washington when Fritz and Jerry dropped off the kids so they could get married and have a short honeymoon.

Other vacations all included staying at little cabins on lakes and fishing for trout. There were lots of fishing stories in my life. Fritz was a member of the Poggie Club in Seattle, which was a salmon fishing club. When I was ten, I got to attend a Sportsman's camp for kids at Fort Lewis near Tacoma when I was in fifth grade. I did not know one person there, so it was a very big growing up experience in my life. We had to sleep in army barracks in cots with a bunch of strangers. We learned archery, shooting rifles, canoeing, fly fishing tying, and all kinds of other outdoorsy activities. We had to work in the kitchens peeling potatoes and washing the dishes just like soldiers. Then I had to come back and do an oral report to all the Poggies at their meeting. It made a huge impact on me. I just thought I was so grown up. I sort of felt like I'd gone through Boot Camp!

Later, Fritz and Jerry bought a 28 foot Grandy Cabin cruiser, which they docked in front of our Mercer Island home. We would take it out through the locks at Ballard, and out into the Puget Sound on weekends. I remember one time we had to go through Deschutes Pass during a very bad storm. I thought we were all going to shipwreck and die. But somehow, Fritz was a star and navigated us though just fine. I just sat inside coloring in the coloring book all through the storm trying to stay calm.

The picture below is me with my two brothers when I was about two years old.

How did you get your first job?

I started working when I was ten as a babysitter for one of the little boys on our street on Mercer Island. I would babysit him for the next few years on Friday and Saturday nights. I remember having to wake up at 5AM on Saturday mornings after babysitting so that Mom could drive me down in the dark to the ski busses at North Mercer Junior High by 6 AM.

I was a worker from the time I was little. I thrived on having a job and spending money, and went on to pretty much had some kind of part time job almost all the time during my teen years. When my friends would leave junior high school on the bus and go home and do homework or watch tv, I would walk myself over a couple of blocks from school and help a young mother with two kids, washing clothes, ironing, doing housework, folding clothes, and generally being a mother's helper.

When it was the summer after 7th grade, I got a job at a neighbor's house on Avalon Drive answering the phones for the father's construction business. When I wasn't answering the phones, I was doing their housework and yard work. Even though the family had two teenage sons they hired me to be the household helper. I always wondered where the sons went, and why they weren't working as hard as I was! It was pretty smart on my mother's part to allow me to have this job, as it kept me really busy every day and trapped in their house so that I couldn't get into any trouble over the summer!

I had the typical jobs, working at restaurants and fast food joints when I turned 16. Lots of funny memories of working as a waitress at a Sambo's Restaurant in the industrial part of Seattle. I would forget to turn in my orders and I would have to run up to the grumpy chef begging him to put mine in the front of others, as I watched my customers scowling at me wondering why their food was so late!

Another pretty funny job I had when I was 17, just out of high school. I had moved into a crummy apartment in the Beacon Hill area of downtown Seattle because I wanted to experience "real life", not just living on a sequestered island suburb. I started working as a secretary/stenographer in downtown Seattle for an engineering employment agency just around the corner from the Pike Street Market, and was taking college courses at Seattle

Community College.

This job was my most memorable, the one that would change my life. There were only two of us working in this office, and the other one was the straightest Christian girl I had ever met! She was always reading Christian books and trying to get me to read them too! She didn't take shorthand, but I did, so our boss, who had to be 70 if he was a day, would have me take dictation in his office on my steno pad, just like in Mad Men. He was the kindest old man, who would talk really slowly and make sure I had enough time to write down all the words and symbols before I had to read it all back to him! I can just imagine what the scene must have looked like, me taking my job so seriously and him being so kind and understanding of all my obvious mistakes! And we had to dress the part, looking like all those other prim and neat secretaries in all those surrounding high rise buildings, and then every day come in to do my drudgery of typing on those darn old fashioned typewriters!

He was so incredibly patient with me. This was before Selective IBM self erasing typewriters. If we made more than two errors in typing a page, we would have to start all over, as the mistakes would show and look badly. I lasted at that job only two months before I confessed to my mom and dad that I was miserable trying to support myself. I begged them to help me get out of the rut I had created for myself, and told them I would go to any college, anywhere, as long as I could quit being a secretary!

Within two or three weeks I was off the Washington State University to attend my freshman year. I never wanted to be a secretary ever again!! What a bore! Off I went to Pullman, Washington, on the Eastern side of Washington State, as a brand new freshman living in Colman Hall!

Ditched by Gordy

This is by far the funniest story I remember from my high school years. I was a Sophomore, fifteen years old, and just beginning to date and go to homecoming dances and proms and such. I was fortunate to have been picked as the Homecoming princess for my class, which meant I would have my picture taken with the other royalty, and I was feeling pretty great about that. All of us were trying to land dates with the stars of the football and basketball teams.

Finally my big chance came when the center of the Varsity basketball game, Senior Gordy M., asked me out!! I wondered how I would even be able to carry on a conversation with him as I barely had ever spoken to him, and he was well over 6 feet tall, and here I was just a shrimp at 5 foot 4!

I immediately started scheming how I could appear more mature and stately! I convinced my parents that I needed new shoes and a new outfit, and immediately started practicing walking for hours in my new taller than normal heels. I tried on my new outfit, and some other older ones, and finally decided on a white button down the back blouse with a flouncy blue and white full skirt. I had to practice even more now that I had my outfit picked out.

The big day arrived and he picked me up after meeting my parents, and we set off to the Orpheum theatre in downtown Seattle. This theatre was historical, multi stories, with a large stairway in the center of the building leading up to the balcony seats. My eyes must have been huge as I stared in horror at all those pesky stairs, wondering how I would ever navigate all those itsy, bitsy steps in my taller than normal heels!

We finally got to our seats way up at the back of the balcony, and I was wondering why he had chosen that part of the theatre. Did it mean that he was going to try and make out with me? The movie was Dr. Zhivago, which was a new release in the mid 60's, and we proceeded to hold hands and chat quietly as we watched. The movie lasted forever, I think it was over a two and a half hour movie, and I thought it would never end! I was so bored I thought I could die, and eventually my boredom must have gotten the best of me and I fell asleep!

I slept through to the end of the movie and Gordy must have been so ticked off!! At the end, he sort of jabbed me in the arm and woke me up. I was horrified to find out what I had done, and he started off out of the aisle with me following behind in a semi-sleepy state. We got to the top of the stairs and he just took off down them without a care about whether I was following or not! Of course, you know what happened next!! My slippy shoes caused me to trip very near the very top of what was at least 25 steps down! And I didn't just fall a few stairs down! I took a full on all the way down tumble, with my flouncy skirt flying over my head and showing my undies, and kept on falling and falling until it seemed I would never stop! When I finally landed in a heap at the bottom of the stairs, I searched while I was still sitting on my butt at the bottom of the staircase, looking all over the lobby to find Gordy, who I hoped would come lift me to safety and rescue me!

He had left! No where could he be seen! He must have been so disgusted with me that he just took off and went home alone, stranding me at the theatre. I had to call my dad on the theatre phone to come to downtown Seattle, get him out of bed in the middle of the night, and come rescue me!

The best part of this story was how much fun I had telling every single Sophomore, Junior, and Senior girl that I could find the next Monday at school what he had done to me! We acted like a hive of bees telling the story over and over, and thoroughly humiliating him with his impolite actions and lack of manners!

He paid the price by finding it very hard to find a date again for quite some time!

Why I Became a Secretary

When I was growing up on Mercer Island in the 1960's, most of the mothers were stay at home moms. On our block on Avalon Drive, there may have been two or three working mothers, and my mother was one of them. I know it seems hard to believe, but women were still encouraged to become mothers and housewives as their main occupation. If a woman did go to work outside of the home, the only really acceptable jobs were secretary, nurse, teacher, nun, or bookkeeper. That truly was the world I was raised in.

I remember distinctly the mothers in our neighborhood taking us to the Mercer Island Fabric Store to help us select fabric and patterns so they could teach us sewing skills when we were only nine and ten. During the summer months, these same moms spent their days laying on towels and watching us frolic in the lake water, while they unwrapped sandwiches and handed out bags of chips and juice. They'd all gather on Friday and Saturday nights with their husbands at each other's houses and have cocktail parties with handmade appetizers. That's what I thought was maturing and growing up.

The other major influence on my life was academics. I wasn't encouraged to be a great or even a good student. Lots of times my family would joke and call me "The Little Dummy"! I know that is hard to believe, but it was the truth. I hardly ever recall anyone ever encouraging me to do my homework. It was just sort of assumed that I knew what my responsibilities were at school, and my parents just were busy with their own lives, and I was supposed to take care of my own goals and aspirations. That included being self motivated to do my own homework and schoolwork to the best of my abilities.

The real test was when the Beatles, Rollings Stones, Herman's Hermits, and Paul Revere and the Raiders came into vogue. I had an old fashioned box type turn table in my bedroom, and I would play 33 rpm albums and 45 rpm singles until they were practically worn out! I became a true Beatle maniac!

When they came to the Seattle Center on August 21, 1964, I was 14 and blond with long hair and bangs and I fit right in with all the other 14,300 screaming maniacs! Woolworth's Department Store sold Beatle wigs, trading cards, and Beatle Bobbin' head dolls! They ran ads that proclaimed, "It's a mad fad, dad!"

Then when the Rolling Stones came to town on December 2, 1965, performing to 8,400 adoring fans, I had my first sex education class right there up on stage with Mick Jagger bumping and grinding to the tunes! When he sang "Satisfaction", their chart-topping hit and closer for the evening, the crowd went beserk. A half dozen fans tried to rush the stage. All of a sudden before my eyes, I knew what grown ups were talking about when they referred to sex.

Prior to that time, my only sex education was walking home in the woods with my friends. We would take our Peyton Place paperback novels, after we covered them with brown paper bag book covers, and read chapters to each other aloud in the woods to try to figure out what sex was. If we came to a really juicy scene, we would help each other try to figure out what was going on, and what was going to happen next. Junior Highs back then just did not teach us anything about growing up except menstruation.

One time, I remember that one of my favorite groups, The Standells came to town. They were famous for the song "Dirty Water" and I was all enraptured with them. I convinced Fritz to take me and a couple of girlfriends to some out of the way teen age nightclub in a whole different district in town. Poor Fritz! We had promised him that we would meet up with him at a designated time. But of course, we were so enthralled and having such a wonderful night, we didn't want it to end. So even though we could see him inside the nightclub looking for us at the appointed time, we kept ditching him and running through the crowds of maniac like teens, hiding and scattering every which way to evade him, until he finally caught up with one of us and insisted we stop our shenanigans. I really was horrible to my loving and so generous step-father that night! I still feel guilty about it. Sorry Fritz!! Please forgive me!

Anyway, to get back to why I became a secretary. When I was in Seventh and Eighth grades, fashion was our main focus. Petti pants which were lacy long shorts- type underwear, which we wore under our skirts, were all the rage. Also stretchy matching tights and turtleneck sets were also in style. These matching sets came in all different colors, and were colorfully decorated with little flowers, polka dots, stripes, circles, and all sorts of patterns to distinguish them from one another. They were all very mod and something like the famous model Twiggy would wear.

The girls in my group used to get to school in the morning and switch outfits with each other in the bathroom so we could try out different fashions. It got so out of hand that the principal had to do something. They made an Executive committee of students to discuss and set up some boundaries and rules for Dress Standards. I self nominated myself for the position of the leader, and actually was chosen by the faculty and won. But I think they only chose me because I was rather popular and chatty, and they wanted someone that the other kids would listen to. But even so, when I had to make my speech in front of the school, one of my best friend's mom and dad told me that I had the beauty, but their daughter had the brains, so I should listen to her ideas as I made up my speech! I kept getting messages from the world that I wasn't that bright, and that I should be more dependent upon others for intellectual help.

When I went to High School, and had to set up my class schedule, my mother and father told me to not worry about going on the college prep track. They said, "Oh, honey, don't worry about college, just become a secretary!" They encouraged me to sign up for all the secretarial courses like typing, shorthand, bookkeeping, and to forget about the humanities and history courses that were on the college prep track.

They said I wouldn't have to work that long, that I would meet a nice man and get married. I figured they knew best, so that is what I did. But you know from my previous writings, that didn't exactly work out the way they had planned. My first job as a secretary was a total bore, and I only lasted two months before I begged my parents to let me go to college at Washington State University!

Precarious Times in Mexico

This happened in the summer after my Sophomore year of college at Washington State University, in 1971. I saw an advertisement on one of the college bulletin boards for
a summer school program for Art and Spanish classes at the University in Guadalajara. I was yearning to do something adventurous over my summer break, and I really wanted to improve both of those skills in a non-threatening atmosphere! Perfect!

I found another ad on the same bulletin board asking for riders to accompany students to the same school. I contacted the driver, made my arrangements with the college, and off I was on an adventure of a lifetime!

We all smashed our meager belongings, mostly backpacks, into the back of a VW bug, and the German engineering student, who was to be our driver, an a couple from Chile, also students at WSU, and myself, all piled in and took off on our adventure from Pullman, Washington.

I don't remember needing a passport to travel to Mexico at this time, just our driver's licenses and student identification cards were sufficient. The driver bought car insurance through another company for the Mexican driving portion of the trip, and guess what? He was going to need it!

We made our way down to Nogales, Arizona, and luckily the husband from Chile could speak Spanish fluently. The Mexican Border Guards were claiming that I appeared to look like a run-away student that they had received notice for, and they were not willing to let me into Mexico. Eventually, he bribed them with some cash and they relented and let us in. That was the beginning of our first mishap in Mexico!

I remember how run down the country side looked, I had never experienced such poverty before in my life! So many kids running around on the streets without shoes! Such hot weather and bumpy roads! Luckily, none of us were experiencing Montezuma's Revenge (dysentery) yet, so we made our way down to Mazatlan within a couple of days. I felt safe and secure as long as I was with my fellow students! We wanted to stop for the night at a motel in Mazatlan to get a refreshing night's sleep, but our driver was in a hurry to get to Guadalajara, and he reassured us that with a little caffeine in his system, he could get there, nothing to worry about.

This is where my trip could have taken a very different turn. I felt in my gut a foreboding feeling that I should not go with them the rest of the way. I felt strongly that we shouldn't be driving at night. But, because I felt so safe with my fellow students, I let the group decision affect my judgement about the situation and went ahead with the group. I wanted to get a room in the motel and get a good night's sleep, which we all needed so badly! But, traveling alone to get to Guadalajara, which was about three hours away, just didn't seem safe either.

So, off we set across the mountain pass that connected the two cities, around dusk, it was not quite nighttime yet. However, you already probably can guess what is going to happen next! Sure enough, nighttime darkness fell, and our driver was getting drowsy at the wheel! Plus, we were noticing that the fields did not have fences, and there were animals grazing just off the roads! There was nothing to prevent an animal to cross the road in the dark of the night! And one did! We ran smack into a burro! He bounced on the hood of the car, and the force pushed him partly onto the roof of the VW bug, and his head was above us, right where the skylight was! The driver had damage to his eyes when his glasses cracked from the impact, the windshield broke with the thrust of the burro hitting it, and I was sitting in the front seat, all messed up!

Remember, this was before cell phones, or any emergency alert system. We were way out on a country road, no town within sight! No flares in the car to use to alert another car coming towards us! I don't remember being conscious at all, as I had cuts all over my face from the windshield breaking, and some of my teeth had been damaged too.

All I do know is that somehow the Mexican police found us, and got us to the nearest doctor's house. The only medical facility around was far, far away, so the best bet was to get us to this doctor's home, where he had a make shift "hospital" set up in one of his larger rooms off the back of his house. He "patched" us up the best her could, but unfortunately this is when I ended up with a horrible case of dysentery and dehydration! Not only was I woozy from the impact of the accident, but now I could not keep anything in my stomach, and was hardly able to make it to a restroom! After several days in this state of affairs, the doctor must have realized my serious state of illness, and had me taken, alone, in an ambulance to a Guadalajara Hospital. During this entire illness, nobody in my family was ever made aware of my situation!

Finally, once I made it to the Hospital, the University in Guadalajara got involved. Finally I had enough wits about myself that I could talk and reason a little bit, and explain that I no longer wanted to stay in Guadalajara for medical attention for my facial wounds. I reasoned it would be better to just skip the University program for the summer, and get home to the States and get fixed up!

Unfortunately, I could not get a direct flight back to Pullman, WA. I literally had to take about five to six flights/ bus rides to get back safely!

I'll never forget walking up the pathway to my little cabin off the park in Pullman, and opening the door to see Mike inside. The look of shock on his face was something I never want to remember! He didn't even know I was coming back, and I had a lot of explaining to do!

Mike's Epiphany

We had already been married in a Universal Life Church ceremony in the backyard redwood forest of one of Mike's best friends in Santa Rosa on August 29, 1971. We had written our own vows, taking passages from various hippy books that were in vogue at the time. Sitting around our little shack of a house in Pullman, Washington, and listening to multiple records by Cat Stevens, we had composed a suitable set of marriage vows that would seal our commitments to each other.

It wasn't long after we had married when Mike and Bob, his best buddy, went on a fishing trip to a lake in Eastern Washington. A miraculous thing happened on this trip! Mike came back and reported that he had seen a vision of Christ walking on the water. And he was speaking to him, saying, "How much do you love me? How much do you love me? Feed my sheep! Feed my sheep!"

He came home and told me the story, and said that we had better go down and buy some Bibles! There happened to be a brand new

Christian book store in the downtown area of Pullman, so naturally that seemed to be the best place to go. We were greeted by Jim Wilson, who would go on to become our pastor and guide in our new walk with Jesus. Mike and I walked in, told him the story, and he asked if we personally had a relationship with Jesus. Both of us had been raised in churches, and had some knowledge of what Christianity entailed, but we had never been asked a question like that, such a personal yes or no question.

At this point, Jim proceeded to explain Christianity to us in a way that we had never heard before, that it was an act of faith, believing that Christ had died for us personally, to give us forgiveness for our sins, and that by accepting this forgiveness we could enter into a personal faith relationship with Jesus as Lord of our lives. We both accepted Jesus in that little store, and went out with new Bibles in our hands, with an invitation from JIm to come to the Campus Christian Center each day at noon for a Bible Study with other believers.

We did attend those Bible Studies, starting with the book of Galatians, and Jim and his wife Bessie would teach the various books of the Bible in ways that we had never heard before. It wasn't long before we were attending prayer meetings at their home in Moscow, Idaho, and services at a non-denominational evangelical church in an old rural outpost near Pullman on Sunday mornings. Little did we know that after eleven and a half yers of marriage how fragile that faith could become, and how splintered and shattered our marriage would then be. But at that moment, we were bursting with new life and new found joy. Below is a picture of us at our hippie wedding in the Santa Rosa mountains.

The Finger Story

This happened in the month of December, 1973. We had a hippie wedding, the summer before, in the woods of Santa Rosa, CA after my Junior year of college. Mike was finishing up his graduate work in clinical psychology, and I needed to finish up a few courses at Portland Community College to get my Bachelor of Arts degree in Humanities.

Mike and I had been living in Portland, Oregon while he finished up his psychologist PhD internship at the Veteran's Hospital. I was just finishing up a few courses at Portland Community College, to complete my final few credits needed for my Bachelor of Arts degree from Washington State University. I was still studying and going to classes, working as a server at a Fish and Ale Restaurant, and working part-time as a roving sales clerk at Meier and Frank Department store at Lloyd Center. Just a few things on my plate, as I would find would be my normal pace of life as a mom - to- be! At this point, I was not yet pregnant with

Josh!

It was December 15, and the Christmas shopping rush was full in swing at Meier and Frank. Sometimes I would be assigned to Housewares, sometimes the Main Floor, and this particular night I was assigned as my first time to work in the Toy Department. Everything was going just fine, and I was at the cash register checking out people with no incidents. Finally, a disgruntled customer was buying a devil doll for his child, and when I went to ring him up, he demanded that I find a box for the doll before he would leave my line! He became very insistent, and in my haste, I said I would be right back and went to the back store room to quickly grab a box off the high top shelf!

I had noticed the boxes earlier in the evening as we had been doing some stocking of shelves. No one else was in the back room with me, so I just got up on a tall stool and reached for the box, and because I was in a hurry I just jumped off the last few rungs of the step stool! Unfortunately there was a sharp edge on the metal shelving and my gold band wedding ring got caught on that sharp edge! My entire body weight was hanging from my ring finger! Eventually, the weight of my body caused the ring to bend, and while doing so, stripped the skin off my finger to the point that it was bleeding furiously, and the pressure finally was loosened when the ring bent that my body was released and fell to the floor!

By this time, my body was in full-on shock and I was bleeding quite a bit, and I walked right past my co-workers and the man with the devil doll, and while a stream of blood followed me, proceeded to get to the women's restroom, never asking anyone for help! It was nearing closing time, maybe 7 minutes away from 9 PM and I was so in shock I was walking around zombie-like, trying to fix my hurt finger! I put it under the running water in the sink, thinking I could clean it up and wrap it up I guess. Just then a very boisterous and loud African American woman emerged from the restroom stall, saw me and my blood all over the floor, and screamed out, "Lordy Jesus, help this girl!"

Had she not come and helped, who knows how long I may have been in there alone, especially because it was nearing closing time! She was able to quickly rally all the help I needed. I remember greeting Mike as I was sitting in the wheelchair, as they were wheeling me out to the ambulance, and said to him,"Sorry, Mike! I really blew it this time!"

The next thing I remember was the doctors working on my hand in the surgical room, and even though they brought in a hand specialist, they were unable to correct the damage that had been done to my hand! And they had the audacity to be discussing their recent golf games while working on my surgery!

I'll never forget the shock and sadness when I looked down at my hand with a huge white bandage, where the bottom half of my left ring finger was gone! And the horrible maze of ugly black stitches surrounding the surgery when they finally took the bandages off! I was no longer able to easily play the guitar and the piano like I used to without a lot of struggle and modifications! Even typing on a keypad was going to need changes in the way I did things for the rest of my life.

I did try consulting an attorney to see if I could get any kind of settlement from Meier and Frank. I don't really know if he was competent or not, but he said I did not have a case. Since it was an "industrial" accident, I could still sell toys and ring up a cash register. He didn't think I had a case, so I never got a second opinion. Meier and Frank gave me only a $500 check for my personal injury! I've often wondered why I didn't get a second opinion.

The funny thing is that while I was recuperating in Portland for the next few weeks, Mike tried so hard to make me feel better. He cared for me so sweetly and was very kind. I ended up with an even bigger surprise in the next few months ahead!

One of my final courses I had to take was a Backpacking class for a PE credit. It was about late February by this time, and the weather was good enough to complete the requirement of a 25 mile trip with the other class members. So, I was all suited up backpacking away, and about one day into the trip I came down with nausea and vomiting. It wasn't extreme or anything, but it did make the backpacking trip a bit more difficult!

When I got back home, I just rested and thought that my nausea was due to the arduous hiking, and that it would go away. After resting in bed for about four days, Mike and I decided it was time to go see a doctor. He asked a bunch of questions, including is there any possibility that I could be pregnant? I said, "Absolutely not!" He said, "Well, you are married aren't you?" I was rather shocked when he came back in the room greeting me, "Hi, Mom!" Little Joshie was on his way!

As the years passed by, I had quite a bit of fun playing up the finger injury when I was teaching! Inquisitive students would notice my finger injury within hours of meeting me! Sometimes out of the blue little kids would come up to me at school and ask to see it! Or touch it! Or come up and say that their cousin told them that I was the teacher who lost a finger! Occasionally I would make up a story that I loved swimming and that a piranha had bit it off! You had to have a sense of humor around all those little kids!

Firewood

This story happened in the wild years when we lived on Rock Creek., probably about 1978. Gat E. and Nancy B. lived in the log cabin next door for a couple of winters. Gat was a domineering strong headed, no nonsense immigrant from Germany, a diesel mechanic, big macho man, muscular and a full on working man in every sense of the word. Jolly and festive once he got to know you, he'd do anything for you if you were down on your luck. Six foot four, eyebrows and hair as black as night, hands always looking as if they had just worked a miracle on someone's Porsche. A powerful stride, long lean legs, big black boots. I remember very well the intensity of the power of his mannerisms and general overall physical build.

Nancy could not have been more his opposite. Raised on the East Coast, from an aristocratic family, a debutante from upper class society, her father a medical doctor, her mother a high society volunteer, raised in the best private schools, college educated, "ate from a silver spoon" all of her life. She had met Gat and they didn't get married, but had come out west to be free of all those constraints. She worked as a doctor's assistant at a local medical clinic, and she had that fresh, clean, well scrubbed, no makeup look about her. Her light brown hair always looked like it needed a little trim. I remember it was always dangling down in her eyes, she wore just moisturizer for makeup, just a simple plain beauty. She was like that in so many other ways too. She wasn't fussy about anything, she had this wonderful, care-free attitude about her life, a no-worry, don't get up tight attitude. No strong emotions, even keel all the time, so different from Gat with his intense power! He absolutely adored her. I wonder now if they are still together.

Part of living in Montana each winter was the ritual of getting ready for the cold. Men would let the facial hair grow starting about the end of September, and most men would be sporting full beards by the mid part of October. During the summer, men were polishing and cleaning their rifles, planning their hunting trips, and getting outfitted for the upcoming deer and elk seasons. In the fall, women were making homemade Christmas presents, painting ceramic figurines, sewing sequins on Christmas ornaments, and putting up all kinds of food in the freezer for the winter. Men were powering up and gassing up chainsaws and loading up pickup truck beds with cords of freshly cut wood for the upcoming winter fireplaces.

On this particular day Mike, my first husband, loaded into Gat's pickup and off they drove, with both of their chainsaws, to go their new load of wood. Mike was the passenger, Gat driving. They were gone what seemed to be longer than usual. There was a good reason why... (remember this was way before cell phones!)

Apparently they had the load just about full, the truck bed 3/4 of the way loaded. Gat was finishing up on a log when he must have hit a knot in the wood. Instead of slicing through the log, the chain saw bucked back and jerked back suddenly, his head bent down to give the saw the leverage he thought he needed, and the chain saw blade went flying straight back and hit him just above his left eye, splitting his forehead in half! Mike had to rip off his down vest, drag Gat into the truck, throw the saws in the back of the bed, and race down that windy creek road, all the while applying direct pressure to Gat's head, Gat screaming in pain, no cell phones back then! Just racing towards town one handed driving, the full load of wood shifting and swaying in the back, slipping around corners, skidding on the gravel edges of the road, speeding towards town 35 or 40 miles away, all the while making sure Gat knew he'd be okay, driving frantically, Mike trying to keep calm, get to town, ER room, stitches! They make it!

Gat wasn't quite so proud after that day, and every time Mike ever left to cut wood after that I prayed more than I ever had before. And I knew Gat had been lucky to be with my courageous, and very smart husband that day of his life.

Oil and Honey

This is a memory of 1975. We had just moved to Rock Creek, Clinton, Montana. We lived in a two story A-frame one bedroom, with a loft upstairs, cabin about fifty feet from the river's edge. We lived so far from town I felt like I was an old-fashioned pioneer woman. My entertainment was PBS radio, planting an organic garden near the edge of the river bank, sewing clothes for my son on a new Singer sewing machine, taking long walks in the woods with Josh in his kiddie backpack, and watching the eagles swoop down while fishing in the front yard.

Wintertime was especially gloomy because you really didn't see the light of day until about 10:45 AM as we were so deep in the valley! And then it started getting dark again by 3:30PM in the afternoons.

Sundays were always a very special occasion as we all piled into our pickup and took off for church "in town", meaning Missoula, which was about 25 miles away. Usually we would visit some friends at their homes after church, and then we'd pick up our groceries for the week at the Albertsons on our way out of town. I remember buying a lot of organic brown rice and grains in the bulk bins because in those days it was easier to make a loaf of bread than to go to the store to buy a fresh one. Plus, it just felt homey and smelled good when you lived that far away from real civilization.

We also "put up" our own peaches and pears every summer, pickled the "cukes" with home grown dill, and picked chokecherries and elderberries on the banks of the river for waffle syrup. All the variety of colored jars looked so sparkly fresh and jewel-like in their brilliance! I remember a real sense of pride each time I went into my pantry to gaze at all the food I'd prepared for a later date.

I used to keep my oils and honey in big plastic bottled and gallon glass jars under the kitchen counter because I didn't like to buy them just a bit at a time. That's where this story starts! Josh was about two years old and I was hugely pregnant with Caleb. It was the fall season and just another unspectacular day, Josh and I hanging out around the house together. I remember now that strangely quiet sensation a mother gets when you realize you haven't seen or heard your child for a while, and that thought comes to you, "Why is he being so quiet anyway?"

As I rounded the corner from the laundry room to the kitchen the first thing I noticed was a strangely slowly moving, spreading liquid puddle nearing the edge of the brown braided rug under the kitchen table! At first I didn't have any idea what it could be, and then all of my suspicions were revealed!! There was Josh sitting in the middle of the puddles in all his glory! He had unscrewed the tops off the oil and honey bottles and jars and was in the middle of it all splashing away with the greatest grin of absolute glee! In his little purple corduroy overalls and with sticky translucent mixture of the oil and honey all over his hair, all stuck to his little brown leather shoes, all creeping towards the wool braided rug! So proud of himself, and ready for my look of approval! "Look, Mommy! Look at me, Mommy!"

Which is worse, honey all over the rug or a sticky little two year old "gooking up" your kitchen even more? I remember grabbing a big pot or a dishpan and racing towards the spreading mass near the rug area first, and for a while feeling sick about all the cost of it all going to waste, and wondering what to tell Mike, and sternly scolding Josh, and grabbing handfuls of the muck, and just frantically scooping it all up with my hands as fast as I could, and working so frantically and wondering where to dump it, would it clog up the drains, and deciding it wouldn't!

Finally, I got it enough under control I told Josh to just stay put, and got the bathtub started. Took off both of our clothes and left them in a pile in the kitchen! Now I'm as sticky and yucky as he is, and running down the hallway, holding him in his sticky little glory, and getting us both all submerged in fresh bubbles and the kitchen still a mess!

I really don't know how I managed to clean it all up in the end!

Irrigation Pipes on Rock Creek, Montana

Memory of 1979-80 I still have the small, well worn, little black Bible she gave me. The memories are still clear in my mind of all the intensity of that week, even though the details are a bit fuzzy.

I remember Doris and Jim Ekstrom driving up to the two story cabin we lived in and relaying the information that there had been a horrible accident! They went on to describe what happened. It was something like this. Clione B.'s two high school sons had been out in the field by Danny Ekstrom's hay field changing the irrigation pipes. Apparently from time to time the location of the pipes had to be changed in order to water all the crops effectively.

I remember the Baker family, they were poor, and didn't own any land to speak of. They weren't "the landed gentry", but a struggling family leasing land from someone, probably the Ekstrom's. Well, as the story goes, the guys, both strapping muscular high school football players, farm boys in every sense of the word, had noticed a gopher in one of the pipes. They tried scaring him out and it didn't work, so eventually both of them lifted the pipe skyward to try to shake him out. What they didn't realize was there was a power line directly overhead ! So, when they shook the suspected inhabitant out of the pipe the metal pipe contacted the power line ! Tragically, because both boys had their hands on the pipe the electricity surged through, and they were both instantly struck down and electrocuted!

I don't know all the particulars of what happened then, all I know is that Doris related to me that never in her life had she seen such grief and despair in a person as she had just witnessed in Clione, the mother. Apparently, someone must have witnessed what happened to her sons and had alerted Clione to the situation. She came running down the path from her old farm house. I can just picture her long skirt and apron fluttering, flying around her in the intensity of her pace as she ran desperately trying to salvage her sons' lives! Then she got down on her hands and knees pleading to God in his mercy to resurrect her boys, lying still and maimed before her.

I remember Doris relating the whole scene to me, how she saw Clione beating the ground with her hands, begging for God's mercy, the pain so intense, so unbelievably real, so unmistakenly abrupt. One son did survive but he lost part of his foot, the power surging through the pipe literally just burnt a whole section of his foot right off! The other son could never be revived.

I never really knew Clione, but I had seen her quiet gentle spirit on occasion in the neighborhood and Doris knew her well. I knew I had to do something, my pain for her loss, even as I write this now I feel that connection to her grief right now.

I don't remember what I baked, or what it was, but I remember knocking on her old farm house door, my two little sons at my side, and watching her open the door with the saddest eyes I had ever seen, and I remember saying something like, "I don't know you, but I heard what happened, and I just had to come and tell you that I am so very sorry, and I am praying for you, and wanted you to know how much we all care." I'll never forget how she put down whatever I had just given her and looked at me straight in the eyes, and at my two young sons by my side, and we just reached out and hugged and hugged, and cried and sobbed, and held each other tight for what seemed to be never long enough! I remember feeling the strength that woman still had for her God, and how she was still a woman of faith, and how even with this grief full upon her she did not give up.

And I remember her saying after we hugged, "But why would you come? You don't even know me?" and I just looked at those eyes and she and I both knew why I came.

About a week after the funeral, Clione knocked on the door of my river front cabin. In her hands she had a little black New Testament Bible in her hands. She said that this was something that had been passed on to her, and that she wanted me to have it now. She expressed that my coming over had been so meaningful, that even a stranger would feel her grief and want to help, and how that had helped her so much.

I still have that small black Bible in my dresser drawer, you know that that drawer most of us keep with all of our heart strings, that we keep because of all the strong memories they serve in our lives. But I don't know why I've never passed it on to anyone else - the time in my life just hasn't happened yet. Here, as I recall this on Thanksgiving Day 2001, I say another prayer for Clione and wish her peace, and want to go back and read through that little black Bible once more.

I Lost Josh!!

Memoire from Winter 1977. It was March on a snowy day, near the banks of the Rock Creek River outside of Missoula, Montana. My husband, myself, our two and a half year old son, and one month old baby, were living in the middle of a five generation family thirty miles east of Missoula, near Clinton, Montana.

Joshua, my oldest son was full into his "cowboy" stage. It didn't matter where he went or what time of day, he wanted to wear his cowboy hat, cowboy boots, and walk and talk like all the cowboys he saw around him. Well, it stood to reason as he was surrounded by several neighbors that made their living on their ranches, and his dad and his best friend across the road all dressed like that every time they were "on the creek". Dad worked as a clinical psychologist, giving pre-surgical therapy to open heart patients, lonely housewives, and veterans of the Vietnam War who happened to need his attention that particular time in their lives, at a medical clinic in Missoula each Monday through Friday. Caleb was about three weeks old, a sweet, chubby ball of joy, who thought his big brother was the apple of his eye. He already had figured out that he was the one who would give him most of his childhood education.

Just across a snowy pathway, in another hand-built log cabin, lived my friend Karen, her husband John, and their little son Jacob. She was pregnant with her second son. She tidied up her house non-stop each morning, and every time you walked in her home it felt like you were transplanted to the East Coast of upper state New York, with all her traditional Ethan Allen furnishings and home spun decor - it seemed like her home always smelled like she'd just polished the furniture with lemon oil. I remember looking through her windows as I was out on a walk past her home, and wondering how in the world she had that much time or inclination to clean so much! My house, on the other hand, was filled with the furnishings the landlord had grown tired of, and gratefully let us inherit for the time we rented from her. It worked for us! And I didn't polish!

On this particular morning there was a light dusting of snow and Josh was just aching to get out and play in it. Caleb must have had a bit of a cold, or maybe he just wanted to nurse, but whatever the reason I just didn't feel like bundling up all three of us to go out in the snow. So, after Joshua's persistent begging I finally consented to letting him go out in the front yard for a while, and I promised him I would watch him. So I got him all squared away with his little brown Winnie the Pooh snow boots, brown snowsuit and mittens and hat, and watched him as he went out to check out the snowy day. All the while smiling and waving to him as I held Caleb to my breast. I pondered how I could be so blessed to have such an idyllic life.

He ventured out a little farther away and eventually wandered over to Karen's front yard where Jacob now had his nose to the window and was waving at Josh. All the while waving and smiling, I eventually saw Karen come to the door and talk with the two boys, and watched Josh walk into her house. Never considering anything wrong, I waved to Karen as both boys followed her inside, I thought to go play.

I remember feeling so unfettered and so peaceful that I sat down and gently settled into the couch to continue nursing Caleb. He eventually went to sleep, and I remember getting a few minor chores done, and then thought..... "Oh, I better call up Karen and check on how the boys are doing - maybe they could come over here to play for a while.." All this peace was thirty seconds away from abject panic!!!

I remember ringing up Karen and questioning .. "So how are the boys - would they like to come over here for awhile?" Then she answered ever so curtly, "Oh, didn't Josh come home? I sent him back at least a half an hour ago - isn't he with you?"

You have a crystalline view of times like this in your life, when you have realized your worst possible imaginings coming true. I remember throwing on a coat, putting Caleb in his bassinet for a nap, and then running in abject panic up and down the banks of the river wildly looking for his little drowned body!! The panic I felt could not be described. Finally after about five minutes of sheer frantic searching, I returned to the front of Karen's cabin and realized that his sweet little footprints were still ahead of me in the freshly fallen snow. Thank God I could see them dimly through the fresh flakes now falling. Oh my God, I could follow them if they didn't disappear! Maybe he was still alive! Oh my God, please make them last.... going over the little footbridge over to the left where Dusty the horse nibbles on our snacks of carrots and hay we almost daily fed him, over to the barn where Bessie the milk cow waits her morning visit, the chickens where we watch Doris as she gathers the eggs, back across the snowy path to the driveway, to the side road and the mailboxes and the bookmobile, and all our travels he and I know so well!! .... His footprints are still visible, oh my God, how is Caleb, I can't stop to consider, have to keep finding Josh, maybe I have hope - across the main two lane road now .. footprints still I'm following, oh my God, I think I see him, he's on his way to Bob's house, I've found him, oh my God he's not drowned, oh my God, I'm lifting him up, his cheeks are so icy cold and so red and moist and soft and adorable! Oh my Lord, can he see the panic I felt, and the relief I now have, the joy welling up inside me, he's alive!!

Never have I been so relieved, but at that moment in time little did I know that how many many more times I would feel fear for my son's safety in his life...

Thanksgiving on Upper Rock Creek

This memoire is from about 1978. We still lived on the banks of Rock Creek and had befriended a Christian family who lived at the very isolated part of this road, at least six miles up from where most of the civilization was. They had two young sons, and the husband and wife had either built their own house, or had purchased it, I'm not sure which.

But this house was completely without any electricity, gas lines, or other labor saving amenities. It was located in a huge field down in the valley where a lot of sunlight lit up the windows of the house during the day time, and there were no other houses near by.

They invited us to come to a completely home cooked Thanksgiving Day, where the turkey and all the other embellishments would be cooked on a wood fired stove. It was a typical cold, snowy day, but I remember the sky was blue and it was breathtakingly fresh and crisp outside.

We all worked together to make a completely delicious meal, primarily cooked at their house, with a few side dishes I had contributed that I had pre cooked at home.

When the natural lights faded and night began to creep in, we entertained ourselves with conversation by gas lanterns and stories for the kids. It was like going back in time, a full century!

I recall being very thankful to get back to my little cabin on the side of the river, and all the electrical comforts of home.

More Rock Creek Memories

Memories of Montana, 1978. Doris and Jim Ekstrom owned a huge chunk of land at the base of Rock Creek, in Clinton, Montana. The built and owned the StageStation RV campground and Restaurant and Bakery, and Rock Shop. Jim was a general contractor, so he built and maintained three rental units right on the river bank, in close proximity to his own homes. We were fortunate to rent the biggest of the three rental units, a large A-frame, starting in 1975 through 1978. They had a great grandmother, Doris and her husband, Doris and Jim's children and grandchildren, (so five generations) all living within a two mile radius of each other.

Doris and her daughter and daughter in law were always busy "putting up something" for the winter, and because I was their neighbor, they felt it was their duty to make sure I knew how to do the same! Blackberries, chokecherries, and elderberries were gathered from the river banks, Native American style, to stir and simmer on the stoves, and cover with melted paraffin for jams, jellies, and syrups for winter time breakfasts.

Peaches, pears, apricots, apples, and strawberries were purchased in wooden crates from local farmers, and put up into sparkling, glistening jars for wintertime cobblers, pies, and breads. When these were "in season", any fully acceptable Montana country housewife was putting up her jams, jellies, jars of fruits, after driving out to the local orchards and loading crates and crates of these into her vehicle, and heading home for a long week's of work!

I'd never done this before, so it was high time I learned! Doris invited Josh, Caleb, and I over to her super cozy kitchen to learn the fine art of jelly preserving! I picked up my lot of canning jars at the local K Mart, a huge black water bath canning pot, and wire basket, special tongs and for lifting all the jars out of the hot bath, and paraffin for sealing everything up neat and tidy, and was off on my way to try!

Mike was busy at the same time, getting hunting lessons from Bob S. next door, on the fine art of deer and elk hunting. In addition, we were fishing in the stream in the front yard, and putting away trout in our little refrigerator freezer. It became quickly apparent that we needed to buy a chest type freezer, so off to Sears and Roebuck we went!

I had, of course, a few misadventures while canning. Sometimes my jars didn't seal just right, or sometimes my paraffin wouldn't hold tight. We would just put those directly in the refrigerator and eat them right away. One time, while I was talking on the phone in the hallway, around the corner from the kitchen, the melting paraffin started to flame up, and I had to throw baking soda and flour on the flames to douse them out!

Next came bread baking lessons, which Doris insisted upon teaching once again! But we didn't just use any old flour. We had to use her whole wheat flour grinder, as she would buy her wheat kernels in bulk, and our bread was the freshest you ever saw! Imagine homemade whole wheat cinnamon buns with the cinnamon and raisins just bulging out the sides, covered with homemade butter and confectioner's sugar frosting on a snowy Montana morning!

When we weren't baking, the ladies would gather at each other's houses for Bible studies, and knitting and quilting lessons. Diane S., across the country road had a full ceramics studio, and we would paint the white ware coffee cups and bowls she purchased in town, with all the glazes, and then she would fire them for us! That was my first experience with ceramics.

By the time Josh and Caleb were three and six months old, I had my brand new Singer sewing machine going like crazy, making them little suits for Sunday school and quilts for our beds, and other items for our home, like curtains and placemats.

When Christmas came around, the ladies would share our Lee Wards needlepoint and cross stitch catalogs with each other, then we'd place our mail in orders, and we would gather to sew sequins on Christmas tree skirts, Christmas stockings, and ornaments for the tree.

I'll never forget how great it was to wake up to a freshly made Mushroom Omelet, and buttery toast on a weekend morning when Mike would surprise us with breakfast, as the snow fell down in the front yard, looking out across the icy cold river in front of our A-frame cabin! What a memory!

This picture was taken when Josh was about eight, and Caleb about five, our fishing with Mike, their dad.

Ice Inside the Windows and Calf Milk

Mike, the two boys, and I moved to the Easy Yoke Ranch in Stevensville, Montana when Josh was about four and Caleb was about two. It was supposed to be a ministry with the Missoula Covenant Church. It was a 210 acre farm, with two old farm houses, a large barn, and most of the fields planted previously in barley and hay. We had many planning meetings and three families from the church were going to live and raise our kids there. Our goal was to make it a working ranch for people who needed a safe place to get their lives back on track and get to know the basics of Christian life.

Mike and I were the first ones to move to the ranch, so we packed up all our earthly possessions and moved into a turn of the century farm house that had no central heat, only two Franklin stoves, one in the kitchen and one in the living room.

There was space for a large vegetable garden, about five acres, and plans were made to plant it mostly in strawberries, and other easy to grow crops, which would eventually be sold at the local farmer's markets.

Eventually, one other family moved into the newer house on the ranch, and the other bought a double wide mobile home and lived in that. They both had central heating, whereas our house did not.

Over time, eventually we had a lot of people helping out on the farm, especially in the summers, and we would provide a big farm style lunch for all the people every day at lunchtime. I pretty much was the head cook and dishwasher. Mike continued his private practice at the Missoula Health Clinic as a clinical psychologist, and Dale B. was in charge of the ranch goings ons.

When winter time started settling in, it was clear that we would be going through lots and lots of cords of wood to keep the turn of the century house warm. It was my job to make sure the fire in the living room was stoked up good with logs for the night, and then again in the morning! I had to bolt out of bed and quickly add a few more logs to the coals, then jump back in bed again under the heavy quilts, while we all waited for the house to warm up. Some days it was so cold outside that we could use our fingernails to cut pathways in the ice on the inside of the windows!

Some days it was so cold and snowy, in order to feed the calves in the barn we would have to mix their milk and water in the kitchen in big pails and buckets, and then tie a rope to the door handle so that we could find our way back to the house after our chores in the barn! It was so stormy outside sometimes we could barely see the house from the barn!

One of the farm kids was named Rachel, and she was Josh and Caleb's very best friend. One day Rachel and Josh came back from playing in the barn completely covered with white powder from the calf milk bag. They had taken handfuls of it and were throwing it at each other for fun! They got a big scolding for that one. Many other times we would find that they had climbed up the hay bales in the side shelters, and were throwing baby mice they found down on the ground!

We had to watch the kids carefully near the pigs, because they would love to eat one of their juicy fingers right off if we didn't supervise them!

The funniest story of all was the time one of the cows was out in the field, and then suddenly, without any notice, the ground beneath the cow just turned into a giant sink hole! This unfortunate cow was now sunk down about seven feet from the rest of the ground! There was no way we could get her back up without help! The septic tank beneath the ground had corroded to the point that the metal just gave way while she was standing on top of that area, and she just sunk with the dirt! I don't actually remember how we got her up, but we did!

A bunch of city slickers trying to live on a farm in the countryside of Montana had just a few challenges! Little did we know at that time what a stress this year had been on our marriage. We ended up moving off the ranch with our marriage just hanging on by threads, and moving back to Missoula where we could try to salvage what was left. We were about to discover how much damage had been done, and perplexed how so much misery could be caused by this misadventure.

Caleb and the Witch

When Josh was attending kindergarten at Paxson School in Missoula I got the bright idea of being the room mother. Caleb was only about 3 1/2 at the time.

We lived in a little two bedroom house on North Avenue East, in the university district near the University of Montana. We had a great big park about five blocks away from our house with swings and slides and big trees. Our marriage was entering the final stages of dissolution, and even though we were trying counseling and being civil to each other, our marriage was entering its final months. Mike would soon be moving out, and I would soon be a struggling single mom. I would also soon be entering the most difficult and darkest times of my adult life. The abject loneliness I would experience, and the constant questioning of myself and my identity as a mom would throw all of us into turmoil!

It was Halloween time, and I told his teacher that I would put on a little party for the kids with treats and games and stuff like that. So all morning, after I dressed Josh up for school and dropped him off, I was rushing around getting all the cupcakes made, and the juice and cups and games ready. Finally it was time to get Caleb and me dressed up too!

I started getting into my witch costume, getting all scary looking, and ready with the stuff packed up in the car! When all of a sudden I realized that I hadn't seen Caleb in a while, so I started to call and look for him!! I called and called, looking in all the rooms of the house, down in the basement, in the back and front yards, in the neighbor's yards! I called my best friend a couple of doors over and asked if she had seen him.. but no luck!

Now it was time for the party to start and I knew all the kindergartners and the teacher were all expecting me to show up for the party! I called the school office, and in a panic explained what was happening, and started driving like mad, all while racing around looking like a scary witch searching high and lo for Caleb!

I dumped off all the goodies and stuff at the classroom, and went racing back scouring the neighborhood back and forth on every street searching high and low for my little son!

I finally thought he might have gone to the park, and sure enough, I searched and I think I found him hiding under the slide, looking scared to death! I think he really thought I had morphed into a witch before his eyes, and he couldn't wait to get away from me!

I still don't remember if I ever went back to finish up the party with the kids. All I know is that I had to get that costume off and all the makeup and stuff before I could calm Caleb down enough to look at me again! Poor Caleb!

Lifeguard classes

In the summer after my divorce from Mike, and after eleven and a half years of marriage, I was still living in Missoula as a single mom with Joshua and Caleb. I thought I needed to have some other skills in my tool belt so that I could get a job to support us. I'd tried going back to college to get a Master's degree in Business, and with all the computer programming, bookkeeping, and accounting classes, I decided that definitely was not "my bag" and had given up on that idea. I looked at my current skill set, and thought I liked swimming! So it made sense to try to get my lifeguard certification and that way I could either be employed as a guard, or certified to give swimming lessons.

So off to the main, brand new city pool I went for my first class. We all gathered around the pool for our first session, and I noticed that I appeared to be the oldest one in the group at age 32. We had to show our swimming ability by doing several lengths of laps up and down the pool. Next, they started to demonstrate all the various signs of a person drowning, and instructed us how to determine the best methods to rescue someone in the various situations.

We went to several more weeks of sessions before it was time to get certified. We had learned a two finger emergency signal. This is what we would use if we ever were practicing with a partner, and for what ever reason we needed to be allowed to come to the surface of the pool for air. We took two fingers on our right hand, and used them as a drum, pounding on the arm of leg of the person saving us, to be used only if we ever felt like we needed to come up for air. We had to pair up, and one of us had to pretend to be drowning while the other one tried to save them.

My partner was the biggest guy in the class, a strapping huge muscleman. He strutted over to the side of the pool, and I was going to be the drowning victim this time. After we dove in, and I started acting like I was in trouble, and everything changed for the worse!! While he took too much time trying to help me, I seriously was running out of air and started swallowing gulps of pool water! I realized that I needed to use the safely signal with my two fingers, but he thought I was just acting and he didn't notice my real need!

By the time he actually brought me to the surface as if he had saved me, I was full of gulps of pool water and coughing and struggling to breathe! I was so freaked out I never got my certification, and it took me a while to feel comfortable in a pool again. What luck to get the biggest muscle man in the class as my partner!!

In the months after this class, I ended up taking a trip to Honolulu to meet up with a man I had been dating. As fate would have it, it was on this trip with another man that I met my dear Nick, who would go on to become my second husband. We met on a Saturday night on Waikiki Beach, and after that trip, my life and the lives of my sons changed radically!

After a court visit to arrange all the details of child custody, the boys and I were off to live in the Bay Area of California, and about to start the second chapter of our lives! Nick and I would be married in the back yard of our Santa Clara home in the summer of 1984, and Josh and Caleb would make multiple trips a year to live with their dad in Montana. Little did I know at that time, but 36 years later, I would be sitting in that same backyard writing the edits to this book in the year 2020!

New Start in California

Joshua, Caleb, and I made our way through the snowy and dangerous roads of Montana, Idaho, Oregon, and California to finally arrive in Redwood City in January, 1984. I had arranged a two bedroom upstairs apartment near their new elementary school, and would be starting my new job as a receptionist at Failure Analysis in Palo Alto shortly. We had piled all we could into our small Toyota Corolla station wagon, and I had shipped twenty more boxes by UPS to be delivered in a clump sometime soon! We didn't have any furniture, not even beds. It was time to get going on a whole new life, around the block from Nick's high rise apartment building with a swimming pool!

Nick would come over every night for a shared dinner, and it got to be a habit that he would bring over some household necessities each time he arrived. Soon our apartment was starting to look like a home, with his dining room table and chairs, and his small kitchen appliances, dishes, and more!

One Saturday, Nick and Josh and Caleb were over at his apartment to get some more things to bring over, and Caleb said the cutest thing! He stepped into Nick's almost empty apartment, and looked around and said "Gee, Nick, it looks like you just about gave everything you had to my Mom! Why don't you just come over to stay? My Mom would really like that!" Out of the mouth of babes, there it was. It wasn't long before we moved out of those apartments and bought our house in Santa Clara, where we still live today, 37 years later.

We bought the house as two single people in June, 1984. We had to merge together whatever we had to make the downpayment, and ended up having to charge the groceries for the first few weeks as we had depleted every bit of our available cash. Now Nick would joke with people and day he went from a single bachelor with two British sports cars to an instant family with two kids and a mortgage! We would joke that we did every thing backwards.

Finally, it came time to get officially married. Because we were so new to the area, I didn't have an established pastor or home church, so we decided to get married at the Court House on a Friday, and have a Saturday reception in our backyard. We had invitations printed for the reception only, and sent them out to the guests. But at the last minute, I was able to arrange for a traveling judge to come to the backyard and surprise everybody with an impromptu wedding ceremony!

My Mom and Dad decided at the very last minute to fly into San Francisco for the big day, so the morning of the wedding I had to drive up to the SFO airport to get them. Along with getting all the food and drinks ready for the reception, I was one busy lady! I barely had time to get dressed myself after fixing up my mother's hair, getting the boys dressed, and helping Nick arrange the backyard for the party. I just threw together some pink mini roses from a Safeway bouquet, tied them up with a pretty ribbon, and put on one of the suits I wore to work for the wedding!

Halfway through the reception, the judge showed up at our front door! Nick called everyone to give him their attention, and said the cutest speech. He said that we had done everything backwards, we had met while on vacation in Hawaii, which was like a honeymoon, we had two children before we married, and we had our house and our reception before we got married! Now it was time to make it all official!

Out came the judge in his flowing black robe, surprising everyone, who proceeded to line us all up, my Mom and Dad, my two sons, and Nick and I in the middle. It was like we were all getting married together! Half way through the vows, he asked Nick to put the ring on my left ring finger. Nick just smiled and proceeded to keep putting it on my right hand. The judge was not going to take no for an answer and insisted that it be put on the left hand. I had to raise my left hand up and say in front of all,"It's missing!" In our rush to get everything ready for the wedding, I had forgotten to tell him that I no longer had a ring finger on my left hand! By this time, everyone had already had a few cocktails, and they all burst out laughing with us! I bet they never had seen a wedding like that one before!

We had a honeymoon in Carmel at a condo owned by one of Nick's friends, so we had a free place to stay. But the weather was so cloudy and overcast, after a few days we missed our sunny backyard with the pool, and drove home! August 12, 1984 was our wedding day, and one of the happiest days of my life! Here we are in Bath, England, many years later, on one of our many trips to the British Isles!

Day Care Adventures

After Josh, Caleb, and I moved to California from Missoula, I needed to get steady employment. So I took a secretarial/receptionist job at Failure Analysis Associates. I really didn't love being a secretary again, but I did my best to earn enough income to pay our house payments and help out Nick with the household expenses. I worked there all the way through my pregnancy with Allie! Many times I remember driving down 101 with a bowl on my lap, I was so nauseated!

When Allie was two weeks old, I was really enjoying being at home being a new mom again, and I really didn't want to find day care for her and go back to my job at Failure Analysis Associates as a technical secretary. I decided to apply to get my license as a day care operator, and I took a few courses at the local community colleges to get my certification ready.

So I put a little bitty ad in the local Santa Clara newspaper, and by the time Allie was two months old, I now had three other two month old babies to take care of each day! Eventually, that expanded to six children! By then I was pregnant with Nikki, so I decided to hire an assistant and go for the full license for twelve! So that's what happened..... all the while still attending college at San Jose State University for my elementary teaching credential.

I would study each night after the kids got picked up, after making dinner and getting every one tucked into bed. Up again at 6, with the day care kids starting to arrive around 6:30AM, and I would study a little bit while I tucked them all in for their afternoon naps. I had classes about two or three nights a week, and I did that for at least two years. Obviously, my weekends were full of studies, and there were cribs in just about every room of our house!

You never knew when you would get a surprise visit from the licensing board for Day Care, and you also had to fill out paperwork each week in order to qualify for the free food program for all the meals you served the kids. Added to that, the constant on going challenge of trying to keep decent help when you were paying only minimal wages. It made for a very interesting way to make a living. I used to get hundreds of freshly laundered cloth diapers delivered to the house, and then at the end of the week I would put the plastic bag full of the stinky ones on the porch for pick up!

We had a great big (three rows of seats) station wagon back then, and I would load up to six car seats in to accommodate all the kids when I needed to get out of the house for a minute to do an errand. I remember Caleb was taking summer school classes at Bellarmine High School that summer, and I had to pick him up every day around lunchtime. Of course, I was pregnant with Nikki at this point too. Caleb would just die of embarrassment every time someone in one of his classes would see his mother drive up with all these wiggly kids in the car, and my big pregnant tummy showing to boot! He made me promise that he would be much happier if I would park a few streets over, where no one could see us when he was being picked up!! Poor kid! I guess they thought all the day care kids were his brothers and sisters! Well, Bellarmine is a Catholic High School, so maybe they really did think a woman with all those kids could be possible!

The funniest story about the day care kids happened at ballet class. I used to get the all the little girls all dressed up in their leotards and tights, and carrying their little shoes in their little shoe bags, loading them all up in the car seats! Then I would use a little rope to guide them all into class safely from the parking lot.

One time, Lindsey was late in being dropped off at my house, and she didn't have time for a decent breakfast before class, so I just took a banana along in the car, and she ate it on the way to class. At least it was better than nothing! We were almost late to class by this point! Of course, there I am walking in with five or six little girls, needing to get all of them outfitted with their little shoes on, and trying as fast as I can. All this while the other moms and the teacher are sighing and looking frustrated at my tardiness and obvious delaying of the class time!

I was finally able to get everyone all outfitted up, and in the circle with all the other little girls, when Lindsey looked down at her fingers and yelled out nice and loud,"My sticky hands!! I don't like sticky hands!!" I sort of motioned with my hands for her to just wipe them off on her leotard so the class could proceed, but she wasn't taking no for an answer. She continued to yell out about her sticky hands until I was able to find some wipes and get her back to normal! Just try to imagine the eye rolling and looks that must have been exchanged between the other mothers!! It was truly humiliating. I made sure to always be on time from that day on!! You better believe it!

One last note, one time about twelve years later, I was at a movie theatre in our area in line for popcorn. I noticed a beautiful blonde teenager ringing up the orders at the cash register, and thought some how that she looked familiar! Guess who it was! Lindsey, the banana hands girl! As we visited I told her I would never forget her banana hands, and she agreed, that she would never forget me either! These were the original four kids I raised from two months old!

Earthquake 1989

People say that you can feel an earthquake coming on. There is this calm, stillness in the air, and the birds seem to know something is up and they stop flitting about. Animals have a sixth sense about these things it seems. Well, it was just a normal day in my day care business, taking care of the twelve toddlers and babies in my charge. An uneventful day on October 17, 1989 until about 5:04 PM!

I had just sent home my assistant, and I was in the front yard pushing six little kids on swings and the slide! And I was seven months pregnant with Nikki!

The ground started rolling, literally rolling, like you felt like you were on a trampoline! The kids started laughing and they thought it was hilarious! I really had no clue, but gathered them up as best I could and scooted them into the house! They hobbled along side me, looking like little drunken soldiers! By this point I knew it was an earthquake, as we watched the water in the pool start splashing out from underneath the vinyl rolling pool cover! I successfully got under the table in the dining room, with all the little toddlers nested under my wings to the best of my ability, and started wondered where their mothers and fathers were!

After a few minutes, the rocking dissipated, only to erupt again with a round of minor after shocks! And many more after that! While we were hiding under the table, the pool water had broken loose from under the cover, the redwood deck around the pool pulled apart by the weight of the water, and the huge waves started smashing into the sliding glass windows right by us! Luckily, the glass did not break! Nicholas and Anthony, two brothers under the table with us, decided it was time to have a snack and were begging for crackers. So we just huddled under the table munching Ritz until we heard some parents start to ring the doorbell!

We had some glass objects fall from high shelves in the family room, but for the most part, our home survived the 6.9 earthquake in rather fine form! Nick made it home and checked the gas line, and in a couple of days we had to have the chimney inspected and worked on a bit. The pool and redwood deck would be so messed up that we had to close off the back yard playground for kids for the next few weeks!

But the most concerning worry was that I did not feel Nikki moving in my abdomen. I would sit as quietly as I could to try to pick up a flutter of movement, and I would poke my tummy to see if I could get her to stir, but she was not moving! Otherwise I felt fine, so I figured it was just a nervous reaction to the stress we were all feeling! Eventually, she started moving again, and all was well in the world, once again!

Welcome Nikki!

Now it is just after the Loma Prieta Earthquake in the fall of 1989. I am still caring for twelve toddlers and babies each day, while attending my final semester of classes at San Jose State University to complete my lifetime credential for teaching in California.

The pool area is still being repaired after all the redwood decks were torn apart by the huge force of the waves crushing the pool cover! I have finally recovered from months of nausea due to my pregnancy at age 38, and we are awaiting the birth of our dear Nikki! We decided her name would be Nicole Marie Pound, a perfect blend of Nick's and my names!

Linda A. is helping with some birth coaching and Josh and Caleb are supposed to arrive from Montana for the Christmas vacation to meet their new sister. I am consulting with Linda on almost a weekly basis to see if there is any advice she can give as to helping speed up the due date. I am still driving down to San Jose for my night classes, parking in the 7th Street high rise parking garage, and walking alone to my classes, sometimes timing gentle and irregular contractions during my classes. December 14th comes, and I feel elated when I sense stirrings in my abdomen! We're on the way to Kaiser to have a new baby girl in the family!

The labor is taking too long! I'm walking around the hallways trying to get things progressing! They have me all hooked up to cords and monitors, and finally they wheel me into the delivery room. I'm pushing and struggling and thinking this must be what delivering is like when you're older! I'm obviously not such a youngster anymore! There is a change in nursing staff during my labor and delivery, and the doctors are basically never checking in. The new nurse assigned to me comes in the room and immediately says,"Why are you laying down in that position! Get up and sit more upright! Why in the world would they have you lying down like that?" Thank God for the change in nurses! That made all the difference and Nikki was born very shortly after that!

Believe it or not, I missed some of my final exams for my classes for my credential due to her birth! So my professors allowed me to write some term papers as a substitute assignment, and I worked on them while I was in the hospital, while she was sleeping!

Nick and I decided that now that I had four children, and he had two, it was time to get a tubal ligation. I had attended the required classes at Kaiser and filled out all the paperwork. They said it was a rather easy procedure that they could do a couple of days after delivery. I fasted and did not drink or eat anything from midnight to eight AM waiting for them to call me to the operating room. They called down and told my nurse that they would not have time for me, and that I should just be discharged to go home!

Well, I wasn't going to take no for an answer! I just quietly walked down the hallways, got on the elevator, and found the surgical floor. I asked to talk to the head of surgery, and told his nurse that I would be happy to continue my fasting, not eating or drinking that day until they could fit me in! I explained that I was a nursing mother of four, and that my husband had to just look at me and I was pregnant! I was serious about getting this surgery while I was still in the hospital! Then I quietly just walked back to my room on the labor and delivery floor!

My nurse came into the room about a half hour later, furious and asking me what did I just do!! I calmly explained, and she went off in a huff! But guess what, I was wheeled down and had my tubal ligation that morning, just as planned. When they wheeled me into the surgical room, all the nurses clapped and gave me high fives! I had become a celebrity for Women's Rights!

Nikki was an extremely easy baby, and I got a break from the daycare of all those other kids! I gave notice to all of them before her birth, keeping only a skeletal group around!

When she was about three months old, I had to go back to student teaching so she went to stay at another babysitter named Lily (what a coincidence that our first babysitters had the same name) with some other newborn babies. Lily's daughter, Kathy, had previously been one of my day care assistants when I had all the twelve kids. Now Kathy worked at Kentucky Fried Chicken, and I remember when Nikki started eating solid food, they ate a lot of chicken, mashed potatoes, and coleslaw for their lunches at daycare!

The only real bug a boo happened when I had taken my first teaching position in East San Jose when Nikki was about one year old. I had only been teaching two days, when Lily called me at work and told me that Nikki was covered with a deep red rash! I had to get a substitute for my first week of work because she had come down with Roseola, a typical childhood illness accompanied with fever and a rash! What a way to start my teaching career!

Eventually, Nikki went to Village Campus in Cupertino, and I would drop her off and race to be a Fifth grade teacher again!

One time we were called into the director's office for a conference. Apparently she and another little boy had taken to making it a habit to hide in the playhouse and kiss! We had to have a serious talk with Nikki and the little fellow, and his parents, and the teachers, and the

director! That reminded me of the times that Allie and Julie had been hiding behind the curtains in my living room, and had been playing kissing games with Nicholas and Anthony!

Nikki would cut her own bangs with scissors from time to time, but this was about the naughtiest thing she ever did. We were all thrilled, actually, that she finally had some hair to cut! It seemed like it took forever for her to grow hair! That reminds me of the time one of the daycare kids had her hair cut by another one of the daycare kids, and I had to tell the mother! Gee, I wonder if it was Allie doing the cutting? I don't think I ever really found out who was the culprit on that one!

For the most part, she would sit back like a quiet little angel and watch Allie get in trouble, learning all the while how to stay out of the way when Allie was being reprimanded. (This went on to become a pattern in her life, even in high school, she would be getting into all kinds of mischief that she hid very well from us!)

Allie did a fine job of ordering Nikki around, setting up plays and song and dance routines for them for perform in the living room. For the most part, Nikki did as Allie directed. But sometimes, Nikki would just be at her wit's end and would refuse to do as she was told! One famous line we always remember was when she told her father one day, "Daddy, you're not the boss of me!!"

A funny time happened when Allie and Nikki both came down with Chicken pox when they were about seven and three. We just got a teenager in the neighborhood to be the babysitter, who also had chicken pox, and invited a few of Allie's friends from second grade over, and they all had a chicken pox day care at my house for a week! I got to go to work as usual, and so did all the other moms! It worked out perfectly!

Nick was out of work for a few months when we lived in Cupertino, and we decided he needed something to cheer him up while he was at home all day alone, filling out applications for a new job. Allie and I drove down to East San Jose and found a cute little springer spaniel puppy, put him in a box, and drove home. We picked him because of all the puppies, he was the one who was the most friendly. Allie decided to name him Billy, because she had a crush on a boy in her class with that name!

Nikki went on to pursue soccer, theatre, gymnastics, and dance classes and eventually was on the dance team/cheerleading squads of both Mitty High School and Cal Poly University! She was definitely the easiest of all my four kids to raise, no question about that! Here she is on the far left back row as a Cal Poly Dance Team member!

Adventures with Audrey, our neighbor next door

This memory happened when Allie was about 3 1/2, and our dear neighbor Audrey lived next door. We always visited her and brought her cookies and other freshly cooked stuff. She had a daughter and a son in law, but pretty much most of the time she lived alone after her husband passed away.

We were visiting on her front porch one afternoon, and Allie was balancing on one of her chairs. I don't recall exactly what happened next, but Allie went flying down off the chair and hit her front top baby tooth on something, and blood started gushing out of her mouth! Not only that, but she started screaming bloody murder! I grabbed her up, and ran home as fast as I could, and while loading her into her car seat, noticed that the tooth had been completely pushed up into her gum line, and it was bulging out in the front, looking very, very sore and painful! Once again, this was before cell phones and GPS, so I just went racing to her children's dentist, not even calling them to notify them that there was an emergency coming!

There is nothing like driving, trying to act sane and unperturbed while navigating traffic, and a three year old is screaming her head off as you drive! My nerves were a complete wreck as I grabbed her out of her seat and went running to the dentist offices!

They were able to take care of her right away, but I think we had some behavior charges along with the emergency bill! Her tooth was sort of gray from that day on, and it eventually came out just like a regular baby tooth. But I will never forget the day Allie fell off Audrey's chair! And, I'm sure Audrey's nerves were blown apart that day too!

Another funny story had to do with Audrey's very large, very furry, and very scary looking calico cat! This cat would occasionally sneak into our yard, or climb on the top of the fence between out two yards. Allie was not fond of this cat, and would run in terror if she saw it, screaming for safety and protection from it! Not one of Allie's fav things, for sure!

About this same time, it was about Allie's birthday or Christmas time, one of the two, and I had bought a "Light Dolly" for her. It quickly became her favorite toy. It was battery powered and if you touched her in certain places, she would light up and pulsated with a total light show of various colors, and maybe even played music while the whole light action was occurring.

Anyway, one night we had tucked Allie into bed and maybe an hour or so after we thought she was soundly asleep, (at this time, she was still sleeping in a crib), when out of the blue, we heard a blood curdling scream of terror arising from her bedroom!! I bolted up the stairs in a flash, thinking that some horrible thing might have fallen on her, or lightning might have struck, or some other insanely horrible action might be going on!! Instead, it was just Allie looking totally petrified scared in her crib sobbing and barely able to get the words out ! "Mommy, Mommy, you have to go get my Light Dolly!! Audrey's bad kitty is going to get her!" This was the message that I was finally able to decipher after Allie's broken speech, but her absolute fright had not helped her explain to me what was the matter!!! I left her in her crib, grabbed a flashlight, ran outside in the dark, searching all around the side of the house where Allie had explained that she had left her, and finally found Light Dolly next to the garbage cans!

I made it back to Allie's room, cleaned off the Light Dolly, and put her in the crib with her. All was well again in the world!!

Teaching with Animals

When I was assigned to student teach in a Fifth grade classroom under the watch of a very popular master teacher, I knew I needed some serious reinforcements in order to be effective in persuading the kids that I was fun too! At that time at San Jose State University, any teacher or credential student could "borrow" animals from their Science lab, as long as you were enrolled in a course at their University. I decided this would be a great way to enrich my teaching experiences, all while providing true hands-on stimulating lessons for the kids.

I started out just getting big taxidermy-style stuffed owls, birds of prey, and other smaller, chirpier, friendlier birds (all stuffed, of course). I would photo copy the pages that went with each variety of bird, and try to do lessons on their hunting habits, habitats, skeletal structures, chance of extinction, etc.

At this time, my master teacher lived very near the school, so at any occasion when he decided to, he would say,"Are you okay with being in charge this afternoon?", and he would take off!

I would have to jump through hoops, literally, in order to get the lessons ready and proceed like a professional, with very little warning. So - the taxidermy birds were my best friends! I would scoot out to the car, bring the birds in when the kids were at recess or lunch, hide the birds in the closets at the back of the room! And once he left, I'd teach one of his lessons for a while, and then when I thought I needed reinforcements, out came the birds! It really worked like a charm!

Later, once I became a "real" teacher with my own Fifth grade charges, I continued to have to take classes at SJSU to finish up my credential requirements. So once again, I was back at the Science Lab almost weekly. I would drive over on Monday afternoons after school, get whatever animal was available that week, throw it in its cage into the back of my car, unload and let Nikki and Allie see it for the night, take it back to the car in the morning, and unload it for my students on Tuesday AM! We had king snakes, Desert tortoises, tarantulas, other smaller snakes, iguanas, and more visit our classroom! Then on Friday afternoon, I would do everything in reverse order. Take the snake or tortoise back to the Science Room, get it checked out for its visible health, and go home for a restful weekend.

One time I got the bright idea to visit a Reptile show and actually bought an iguana, proudly bringing it back home. As soon as I got it in the door, my whole family started yelling , "Are you kidding?" Nikki and Allie were scared to death of it, and when I explained that it only ate small bugs and crickets, they ran off in terror. I ended up taking the iguana back to the Reptile Faire, but of course, the guy I bought it from was already gone! So I ended up just giving the whole thing, iguana, cage, food, and water set up to another reptile guy just to be rid of it!

But the funniest time was when the king snake was able to finagle out of his cage in the Fifth grade classroom, and we looked over and he was hiding in a corner. I screamed, "Help me! I'm scared!" and this big strapping Fifth grade boy came to the rescue, grabbed him up with both hands, and saved the day! He yelled out, "Don't worry, Ms. Pound! I've got this!" His status as a macho man in the classroom was increased by quite a large measure that day! I guess I wasn't much of an animal fan after that!

What were you like when you were 40?

I was working as a Fifth grade teacher at R.F. Kennedy School in East San Jose. I started teaching after having a day care at my home for twelve kids after Allie was born in 1985. Then in 1989, our lovely Nikki was born, which made for an interesting work life. How I managed to navigate teaching 32 fifth graders, and raise two little girls at the same time, I will never know!

I'd have to drop Allie off every morning at Bethel School in Cupertino, and get Nikki to either Trudy's day care or Village Campus and get to school by 7:30AM every day! Don't ask me how that all happened. Eventually, we moved to Cold Harbor Avenue in Cupertino and Allie attended Collins Elementary. She had to go to counseling when her kindergarten teacher had a coughing attack in front of all the kids, and a brain aneurism, and passed away! What a year!

My Fifth grade students were mostly English language learners and either Vietnamese or Hispanic. Fortunately Mr. Rice, my principal, allowed us to do whatever we could to reach these kids. We could choose to use textbooks or not. We could teach using whatever creative means we could, including using hands on science to teach basic vocabulary, or teaching by using the newspaper. Computers were just coming into use at this time, and the only computers we had were in the lab where we inserted floppy discs and mostly played Oregon Trail or Reader Rabbit. Basically, everything depended upon my ingenuity and creativity.

I remember Allie started auditioning for plays with the San Jose Children's Theatre when she was in kindergarten. I figured out how to use the costumes from the costume room with my fifth graders to put on several plays. We enacted the Pilgrim Thanksgiving story in front of the whole school, and performed Mexican Cinco de Mayo dances using the vests and fancy dresses and skirts, all from the theatre's costume room. How I managed to get Allie to play practice, navigate all the costumes, and lesson plans, and cook dinners, and grade papers, I will never know!!

I also had two very talented students named Minika and Sara, both from Cambodia, who wanted to try being in a play. They auditioned for Jungle Book and got key roles in the play. I ended up having to pick them up after school and get them to play practice too. Crazy times! I guess the traffic on the freeways couldn't have been that bad back then. Or all this would have been impossible.

Mr. Rice had a huge influence on me as a teacher. He was patient beyond belief, and he was not a micromanager. He allowed us huge creative freedom in our teaching.

I remember one time I really blew it. I was teaching a Fifth/Sixth grade combo class, which was all new to me. I had checked out some videos at the Santa Clara Children's section of the library on Greek and Roman culture. It was a Friday afternoon and I popped one of the videos in for my 32 students to watch. Of course, I had been too busy to preview the video first. All of a sudden the real actors were acting out the Oedipus scene and the mother's breasts were completely exposed on the screen!! I jumped up as fast as I could, threw my body in front of the tv screen, and turned it off!! Then I watched as my students faces were either turning into a jumble of horrified tears or elated joy!!

I calmly said that we were going outside for PE. I knew I was going to be fired for this!! I had to wait until Monday morning to tell Mr. Rice what happened as he had already left for the day on a Friday afternoon. When I recounted to him what had occurred, he merely asked me if I thought any of my students had ever seen a breast before. I humbly nodded my head and said, "Well, I guess they have."

Not one parent called the office to complain. Such were the joys of teaching in a tough neighborhood!!! I sure had a field day taking back those videos to the librarian at the Santa Clara Children's section, and explaining to her my teaching nightmare with all the gory details!!

Camp Campbell

Memoire from 1993. I was teaching sixth grade at R.F. Kennedy School in East San Jose and was still a novice at teaching. Science camp was being held at Camp Campbell, which is located in the La Honda, Boulder creek area off Highway 94 area by Felton, CA. It was my first experience going for for a whole week in the woods with my thirty two students. I ended up learning a lot more about camping and hiking than I ever wanted to!

It began with a couple of days of leisurely activities and short hikes adjacent to our campground. Several days into the week, we were invited to go on the full day hike. Naturally I wanted to see more of the surrounding forests and hills, so I decided to join my thirty or so students and a camp counselor for the day hike.

After a strenuous morning hike of five or more miles, we were all famished and couldn't wait to eat our sack lunches. I remember thinking how good food always tastes when you're in the forest.

Even squished up ham and cheese sandwiches taste like a feast! We had noticed bobcat "scat" on the trails several times during the morning hike, and I thought about how much those little guys would have delighted in a bite of our food!

It was about 3:30 PM in the afternoon and we were on the final stretch of the way back. Because I'd been with the whole pack of kids all day long with their constant chattering and laughing, I longed for some peace and quiet. That's when my problem began. I asked the counselor if I could go hang a little back of the group and make my way back alone. I walked on, quite a ways behind them, but I kept listening for their voices to guide me on the path. Suddenly, I realized that I couldn't hear them anymore!! So I waited, with my ears intensely listening, kind of getting scared at this point, because I couldn't imagine how I could have missed the correct way back!

It was about this time that I realized that I had no extra food, no more water, no flashlight, no whistle, no warm jacket! The sky was getting darker by the minute, the weather was getting colder, and I had no idea which way to get back all alone! I started to run forward on the trail, and then looped around a bend in the trail to see if I had taken the wrong fork in the path! Nothing was working! When I realized how lost I truly was, and how alone I felt, and the woods around me started to spin like I was on a spiraling ride! I had to sit down to calm myself down, and started praying like I had never done before!

Eventually, I figured it was best to try to make it back by myself, even though I had no idea if I was on the right way back. As the darkness increased and the cold was starting to freak me out, all of a sudden out of the blue I could hear voices singing! Aha! I could hear the voices of my dear students far, far away, but clear enough that I could barely tell what direction they were coming from!

I tuned my ears as best I could to the direction I heard them, and raced down the path as fast as I could, running with all my strength and might to get closer to the singing. At last, I was able to hear them much more clearly, and knew I had better slow down my pace so I didn't appear panicked when I finally caught up with them! Naturally, when I saw the whole group I was as relieved as I had ever been in my whole life. I didn't get eaten by a bobcat, and I didn't have to spend the whole night shivering in the woods all alone!

I never let on to anyone about what happened to me until later that night after dinner. I confessed to the camp counselor what happened to me on the trail. I asked her if it was her custom to encourage the kids on her hikes to sing like that on the way back. She said no, this was the first time she ever had a group start singing like that on their own. I know why they started, and I thank God that they did. He really heard my prayers!

Halloween Nightmare at Church

We had just moved to Cupertino into a large four bedroom house, and kept our other house in Santa Clara as an investment. We found a family to rent from us, so we thought it was going to be a good arrangement. But money was tight, tight, tight!! Every time we turned around it seemed like the family was calling Nick about some minor repair that he needed to attend to. Such is life as a double home owner!

Allie was in First grade at Collins Elementary, and Nikki was three and going to Village Campus Preschool. I was working as a Fifth grade teacher in East San Jose, and Nick was working in Hollister, so he had a long commute every day. We had been scrimping and saving in every way we could. At one point, we were so broke that when we needed tires for one of our cars, we bought the ones on sale at Montgomery Wards that were the wrong size just to save money! From that time on, the speed gauge on the car was always slightly off due to the wrong sized tires!

About this same time, we were looking around for a new church to attend. Linda and John A., our good friends, who were former parents of my daycare business, an because we knew their kids well, had recently invited us to attend West Valley Presbyterian Church where they just started attending. We were all relatively new to the congregation, and were just getting to know people. The church was bulging at the seams in those days, and Ron McHattie was the pastor and Martha was the children's minister. Nikki and Allie were enrolled in the Cherub and Joyful Noise children's choirs, going to Sunday School, and we were all attending pretty regularly each Sunday.

This was Halloween season, and because money was so tight, I had shopped for Halloween costumes at some local garage sales, and had quite a number for the girls to choose from. Allie looked at all her choices, and decided that she would like to be a little devil for the holiday. She was all decked out in red, with little horns on her headband, and red tights, and a red skirt and top, and even a red tail with an elastic band that looped around her waist and came out at the back of her skirt! Nikki was in her Princess stage, so I am quite sure that is the type of costume she chose. Who knows? I may have even dressed her as an angel!

This is where the story gets funny. The next Sunday, after Halloween had already happened, the children's pastor called all the little kids in the church up to the very front of the communion table, and they were talking about Halloween. She was going on about how it really isn't a Christian holiday, and wanted the kids to engage with her in a conversation about what they did over the Halloween Night.

Allie wasn't shy at all and when Martha called on her she freely shared with the entire congregation about how she had dressed up as a little Devil! You should have seen the looks on the faces of the people as they turned around to glare at us, her parents! I slid down in my seat as far down as I could go, and I think I may have ducked my head under the seats in front of me, feigning to be looking for something on the floor! We were all in complete embarrassment as the pastor went on to explain to all the children gathered in front of her (while the entire congregation was listening), that dressing up as a devil didn't mean that Allie really was evil, and that even though Christians celebrate by wearing costumes and going trick or treating, it wasn't really okay to dress like that again. She was trying as best as she could to diffuse the embarrassing situation, and also to explain to all the little kids gathered for her inspirational message. I think I slunk out of the back door of the church as soon as I saw the sermon was about to end, and dashed off to my car as fast as I could that day!

Boy, did I learn a lesson about that one! When I got home I think I threw that costume in the trash, never wanting to see it again! I prayed and prayed that God would forgive me, that out of my ignorance and desire to let Allie have her way, I had really made a big embarrassing mistake! Over time, I guess they sort of forgot about it all, but I sure didn't!!

Blue Hair and Blue Hands

This memory happened in the early years of my teaching career during the early 1990's at R. F. Kennedy School in East San Jose. My classroom was located in a run down, very old portable for several months this school year. Remember, it was a year round school, so we had to change classrooms every three months! Several other teachers were in close proximity, and they were all upper grade portable classrooms.

One of these teachers was a tall, foreboding, very self assured Sixth grade female teacher, who had a habit of coming up behind her students as they were working, and startle them! Many of them developed almost a "twitch" from jerking their heads around to see her peering eyes glaring down upon them! I was always secretly glad that I wasn't one of her students, as I felt so intimidated by her too!

Another Sixth grade teacher next to me was one of our Union Reps who had a heart of gold. He owned a real barber shop in San

Jose, and he would race over after school and on the weekends to cut hair as a second career. Often, in the early mornings before school started, you would see kids coming into his classroom way before the bell rang. I found out that he was giving free haircuts to kids who needed them! It was all very secretive and hush hush, and so generous of him. He also would bring bags of clothes in to give away to students, all very secretive so no one would know.

One time I remember having a student who was so impoverished that her shoes were always falling apart. I arranged with her to take her shoe shopping after school, and she got to pick out several pairs that she liked. It seemed like the teachers at our school were always reaching out like this to go the extra mile for our students.

We worked in a very rough part of town. Sometimes we would see gang fights in the surrounding neighborhood, and sometimes we would even see gangs gathering on our playgrounds after school. We were encouraged not to stay late to work when gang tensions were particularly high. Once I had a student whose brother was killed in a drive by shooting in his front yard! We had one teacher at our school who had her pay check cashed two times before she even got to the office to pick it up on pay day! And, she had her car stolen from the parking lot of our school during school daylight hours while she was in her classroom!

But for the most part, this was the school that pulled on my heart strings more than any other, as I was a brand new teacher with so much to learn. And the students were so appreciative of every little extra thing we did to try to encourage them. Most were Second Language learners who had great challenges in learning the curriculum in a new language with very little parental support, as most of their parents were Non English speakers.

I remember one time Mr. Rice, my principal, called me in for a conference after school. He opened by saying he had a problem with one of my students, and we needed to discuss a solution. I was so worried that I had done something wrong, or had offended someone! He went on to explain that Chris P. was very upset and had come to his office to complain! Chris was one of my very brightest students, and I was so concerned as to what could be the matter! He was one of those kids you could tell was raised in a very loving, and affectionate home. He looked as straight as an arrow, and was very well parented by his adoring mother and father.

Apparently he had to leave my class that week, and had attended a special GATE program for an hour or so for gifted and talented kids. He came in to tell Mr. Rice that he was very disappointed because every time he had to go to GATE he felt like he was missing out on some other more fun and exciting lesson that I had taught that hour while he was gone! He wanted the principal to know that he didn't appreciate having to leave my class! We arranged it so that Chris could pick and choose which class he wanted to attend after that.

I used to get so busy trying to make fun and engaging lessons for my students that often at the end of the day my hands would be covered in blue dry erase marker ink from all the erasing and teaching I had done! I had a reputation for being super energetic and creative in my teaching style, and if I thought I could reach someone who was stuck on something, I would quickly erase what was on the board and try to explain it again with a drawing or some other method, like drawing a Venn diagram, or making a chart. I drew a lot of impromptu pictures to help my struggling students understand better with picture clues.

The funny part of this story is that I ran into Chris P. many years later on the campus of San Jose State University. I was working on one of my Master Degrees in Education, and I caught his eye outside of the Engineering Building one day around 4PM after school, as I was racing across campus to get to my graduate level class. Out of the blue I heard a loud voice yelling "Hey, Ms. Pound!" I turned around to see a huge man waving his hands in the air, with a great big smile on his face, and long shoulder length blue hair!

Lo and behold, it was Chris!! He had graduated with honors from high school, and was now studying to be an engineer! We chatted for a while to catch up, but I was racing to get to class so it wasn't a very long conversation. All of a sudden I got the urge to ask him "So Chris, what's with the blue hair?" He chuckled and came back with,"What's with the blue hands?" I held out my hands in front of us, and sure enough, they were still covered with blue ink from that day's teaching! What a great memory this is! Such luck to run into him like that so many years later.

Sword Lake Backpacking

If I recall correctly Nikki was about three, and Allie about seven, when this occurred. We found out about a darling little lake near Strawberry, CA that was suitable for backpacking and camping with kids. The trail to get there was only about 3 miles from the car parking lot, so it wasn't that far! We each had a backpack, all our gear, food, flashlights, sleeping bags, so of course Nick had the heaviest pack, probably about 27 pounds. We planned to stay two nights, and see what happened!

We backpacked on this trail about three times so I may get some of the details mixed up between the different trips. I do know that Nikki was a real trooper most of the way, and when she would get frustrated and bored walking we would bribe her with a Skittle or some other little sweet treat if she would just walk another 30 or so steps! At one point, Nick had to literally carry her sitting on top of his backpack!

Allie was the best at navigating the trail, which sometimes could be hard to find. She would go on ahead a little bit, find the most well traveled dirt trail, and yell back to us that she had found the way. I don't remember her complaining about hiking at all!

Once we picked our campsite and got settled, there was all kinds of adventures to get interested in. I remember a lot of high rocks, and teenagers jumping off cliffs into the lake. Also, water snakes swimming in the lake! Lots of trails that went almost all around the circumference of the lake. Many fallen logs to walk on like balance beams too.

At night, we had to get all of our food wrapped up in a waterproof bag and rig it up high in the tree branches so bears couldn't get into it! I think we heard bears sniffing around our tent at night too! We'd all be squished up in a little three person backpacking tent, listening and trying not to wake up the girls! We were told you couldn't even keep toothpaste or sunscreen or anything in your tent at night or they might try to get in!

Another time, we made plans to go with a Nancy, a fellow teacher at RF Kennedy School, and her teenage son. This trip was way more precarious and scary! I think Nikki must have been cold the last time we came here, so she insisted on taking her heavy padded jacket and long pants, and would not take no for an answer! So her backpack was heavier this time!

Nancy was a pretty accomplished camper, so she inspired us with confidence that this would be a great trip! This time, Daddy wasn't going with us so it was just the girls and I , and I wasn't able to carry Nikki and all the gear too! The weird part was at the beginning of the trail we saw these hunters with bows and arrows on their backs, so right off the bat I was freaked out that they might mistake us for a deer as we hiked through the woods! Luckily, we made it out of that danger safely!

We set our tents up and Nancy impressed us all with her cooking skills. She brought Chinese pork sausages and added them to some kind of broth with rice to make an absolutely yummy dinner. We had an added feeling of safety because her son was with us, to protect us from weirdos! We had noticed some other male campers on the trail, and it looked like one group was toting in a cooler of who knows what?

This is when the story gets freaky. In the night, huge cracks of thunder and lightning erupted, along with a huge rain storm that followed! Nancy said we should move our tents away from the trees in case of lightning, but the only place left was on top of a cliff like place on top of a gigantic granite rock. So that's what we did, moving all our stuff in the dark of night! I absolutely remember Nikki reminding me how much she was right in bringing her warm coat and pants at this point! I think she had the warmest clothes of all of us, as we were all pretty much drenched!

The next day, we could see smoke from the far off mountains, so clearly the lightning had started forest fires in the area, but they didn't appear to be that close, so we just stayed anyway. I think we stayed only one night and that was enough!

Another time we went camping and backpacking there with Caleb and Nikki and Allie and me. I'm not sure if Nick was on that trip. All I remember about that one was Caleb's shenanigans teasing the girls. On the way there, we stopped to get gas, and he paid for and snuck a big red lollipop in his pocket. After we had left the gas station, he proceeded to lick it deliciously in front of them, tormenting them with his great big red lollipop, not willing to give them a try! So, as soon as we reached civilization on our our ride back home, the girls were begging to stop and get some candy! From that time on, whenever we stopped for gas, the girls always made sure they got a yummy treat too!

That reminds me of the time we went hiking at Big Basin Redwood Forest with Caleb. We were all hungry for lunch and we found a hamburger place in a strip mall near Mt. Herman called Chubby's. Caleb must have been in a healthy eating phase, and he refused to eat a Chubby's hamburger. I remember all the rest of us yelling "Chubby's, Chubby's, Chubby's!" to try to get him to change his mind! He ended up getting out of the car and ditching us, and eating some other healthier place, finally to return to Chubby's after we had delighted ourselves with greasy burgers, fries, and other disgustingly unhealthy drinks! From that day on, whenever we are on the Mt. Herman Road, and we see that drive in restaurant, we still yell "Chubby's, Chubby's, Chubby's" as a remembrance of that very funny day!

What is your funniest story about working as a teacher?

I call this the "Girdle Story". When I retired in 2018, it was one of the memories I shared at my retirement event at Bishop School, with all my teacher friends and the main administrators from the District Office in attendance. It is one of my fondest memories of my teaching career.

As teachers, we wear so many hats! Ordinarily I would dress up to go to work because it set the day off right, and it got my mind into a focused frame of mind. It is probably a generational thing, because when we were raised in the fifties and sixties we moved from white bobby socks to real hose held up by a garter belt! We didn't even have panty hose back then, but I always remember wearing a skirt or a dress, so that is what I did most days to go to work. I remember wearing panty girdles even in high school.

Somehow you wanted to be all "sucked in" when you had to walk by the line of guys at the end of the hall, you know, "the gawking wall".

Even as a freshman in college I remember stacking my cardigan sweaters and kilt skirts in my closet, and primping myself with curlers and hairspray and a panty girdle to go to class at Washington State University in Pullman, Washington. We looked like sorority girls that my mom so desired that I would become. But I was alas a "dormie" at Colman Hall, never to be a Kappa Alpha Theta, like she was.

So all throughout my years I've had memories of my mom's girdles in her purses when they got too tight when we went out to dinner, and she would race into the women's room to remove hers. Then she would take the rolls from the breadbasket and wrap them in a napkin and stuff them in alongside the discarded girdle!! I always knew my mom must have had a great dinner out with my dad if her girdle was in her purse when they got home! Her dinner must have been really tasty and filling!

But the funniest girdle story of all happened when I became a teacher in 1991 at R. F. Kennedy School off Lucretia Avenue in East San Jose. It was a hectic morning when I had to attend a training at the Santa Clara County Office of Education, and I was alone in my classroom racing around trying to get the lesson plans and all the details ready for the substitute. On this particular morning, I was dressed in a rather "preppie" style, and as I drove to work I realized that my panty girdle was showing when I sat down in my green corduroy shorts. I knew I would have to take off my girdle before I went off to the workshop. But when I got to school my substitute was soon to arrive and I still had some last minute details to attend to. So, racing around the classroom I realized I better take care of my girdle problem right then and there as I was running out of time! I hid behind my closet door, with one eye on the classroom door, and quickly raced to get that sticky, binding, troublesome article of clothing off as fast as I could! Just about then the office called and said my sub was on his way to get squared away with the day's instructions! I instantly, without hardly thinking, tossed the offending article into a basket of weaving supplies at the side of my desk.... never to be thought of again until I was sitting in the middle of my workshop!

The look on my face must have said it all.... how horrified and panicked I felt! How could I have been so careless? What if the substitute found it? Even worse, what if one of my students found it? (This was before cell phones and text messaging.) The secretary at my school would never understand! What could I do? Who would I call for help? Should I just ignore it, and hope it all faded away? What could I do? Eventually, I figured out that I could call the secretary, and ask her to put the call through to my friend who was the Project Specialist, who worked with kids with reading difficulties, in a room adjacent to mine. I knew she was older and would be a true confidante and friend. I scooted out of the workshop and in a low hushed tone called on a pay phone in the hallway and explained my predicament. She promised me she would wait until recess and then remove the offending article.

The funniest part of all was when I returned to work the next day. I approached my friend in her office and I didn't have to even ask... she merely pointed to a desk drawer , with a scornful look on her face, and said, "It's in the paper bag!" No other word was ever necessary! She never once said anything about the incident to me ever again!

London with Uncle Jimbo

I was working the first ten years of my teaching career at a year-round school. What this means is that you get three long vacation times a year, not just one big summer vacation. I was on Track C, which meant that we started the school year in July, taught a month, had one day to pack up everything in our classroom into a rolling cart, and went on vacation the whole month of August.

Then in September, we had one day to unload all our stuff from our rolling cart, set up our stuff in a new classroom, and teach until December. Then, we had that whole month off. Then in January, we would set up again in a new room again, and teach until April!! There was so much moving in and out of classrooms by all the thirty teachers at my school, it could make your head spin! You never knew where to go find any of your friends after school for a quick chat! We were constantly checking the school map to find one another! Now it is April, and that is where this story starts!

Jim, Nick's brother, had visited our home one night and we were chatting over dinner. He casually mentioned that he had a couple of flights coming up where he was the pilot on an United Airlines international flight to London, and inquired if either one of us would like to go with him on a trip. He could get business class seating for us with his buddy passes! Since I had a long vacation month coming up, I said ,"Of course!" He asked would I rather go for one or two weeks, so of course I said two!

Now I'm all comfortably situated in my larger than normal, upgraded business class seat, making decisions, reading travel guides, and just planning away all the adventures I could have! Unfortunately, Jim had to get back on the plane and fly back to the states in a day or two, and then I would be on my own! A couple of times during the flight, he would have his co-pilot take over the controls, and he would come back and check on me. I would enthusiastically tell him all the ideas I had about all the plans I was making! Now mind you, this was my first real international flight. Up until this trip, the farthest I had traveled was Vancouver, BC and Guadalajara, Mexico. I had never seen Europe before!

Finally, we were in London, and had to go through Customs! I tagged along behind the flight crew, with all the pilots and flight attendants, and we loaded up into a chartered van to take us to the hotel near Kensington Palace, where they all stayed on lay-overs.

This is where the funny part of the story starts! As I gazed out the windows of the van, and my eyes got wider with every dazzling sight I was taking in, I found that I was more and more stunned and shocked! By the time we got off the van and were walking into the hotel, I was completely stumped for words, and could barely stutter! Jim thought something was wrong with my brain, he had never seen me like this! I think I was so surprised to finally see Europe for the first time, I was in a state of shock! Plus, being somewhat jet lagged didn't help. We checked into our rooms, took a brief nap, and we walked down the street for a cup of tea and a little bite to eat. Finally, I could barely start to talk again!

He was a star! He showed me how to buy a pass for the Tube, the London subway system, showed me how to navigate and read all the maps and how to find my way around, took me to see a few famous sights, and booked a room at that same hotel for two more nights, since he had to leave the next morning to go fly back to the States, so that I could get my bearings again! He also helped me find a bed and breakfast in Dublin for a few days, so I could see the country where my ancestors lived! I couldn't have done it with out him! I wasn't much of a brave traveler after all!

The way to see London, in my opinion, is to book Walking Tours with a guide, picking and choosing the sights you want to see. That way you get a great idea of the lay of the land, and you get a professional guide to take you around, and you are not all by yourself, but in a group of interested travelers. So that's what I did. Eventually, I got myself on a flight to Dublin! Now my Irish adventures could begin!

I made a lot of mistakes during my time in Dublin. First of all, I had a suitcase to drag along and a backpack on my back. Next time I traveled by foot, I would learn to take only the backpack! And just minimal clothes. Jim had helped me book a room, but this was before cell phones and GPS! I only had a city map to look at, and I was such an unexperienced traveler, I tried to get there on a city bus instead of just hiring a cab! I ended up dragging my suitcase and heavy backpack all throughout these neighborhoods searching for my B & B at the far end of Dublin! I would have been better off just getting a room right downtown! Live and learn! Eventually I learned the smartest way to get a room for the night.

This is what I learned. Buy a week long bus and rail pass so that you can travel anywhere you want without buying tickets each day. Find out whatever public transportation gets you quickest to the next town, find a room right by the train or bus station, then dump your suitcase and backpack off there for the day, and head out and see the sights. Get back before dark (especially if you are a woman traveling alone), and get a good night's sleep. Never a need to book your room in advance, it just gives you headaches trying to find it! Then head off to the train or bus station in the morning, off to a new town and repeat! I could get by on about $100 a day, traveling from town to town all throughout Ireland, and I had a ball!

I rented bikes, went on tours with other travelers, never had a plan, just traveled like a bird on the wind! I never felt afraid of traveling alone, as long as I was in my room at night before dark set in. If I didn't know where to go next, or if I was in need of some advice, I would go into a pub, order a Guinness, start up a conversation with the ladies at the bar, and by the time I had my beer down, I knew where to head off to the next morning! Sometimes I had a small flask of Powers Irish whiskey in my pocket, and I'd share a bit in the coffee at our lunches with other travelers! Such great memories!

This was all before technology like computers and cell phones and GPS. Now I am sure it would be so much easier!

The "Other" Finger Story

Allie was in Fifth grade at Carden El Encanto Primary School, which was located one block from our home on Fairlane Avenue. She and Nikki would walk to school each morning after Nick and I took off for work, carrying their lunch pails, and backpacks, and gymnastic and soccer clothes, ready for their afternoon practices.

We kept a pretty rigorous schedule those days, before and after school. I figured out about age 40 that if I didn't exercise and take care of myself before work, it wasn't going to happen. So this is when I started waking up at 4:30 AM each day to swim a couple miles at the Santa Clara Swim Center before school, and race off to work about 7:10 to make it to the bell for teachers at 7:30 AM! Allie was a lifesaver for me in those days, making sure both girls had lunches ready, and getting them both to school on time. Never did I get any calls from the office about them being tardy, or anything else.

So I was rather surprised when the Carden office staff called R. F Kennedy School one day, and asked if I could come to the office phone to speak to their principal. I was super scared, but it really wasn't a gigantic emergency! Apparently, Allie had been sticking her ring finger in and out of a hole in a metal pole where her classroom lined up after recess, bored and just seeing if her finger would fit in the hole in the heavy metal, while she waited nonchalantly in line to go back into class.

Well, a little problem happened when she tried to remove her ring finger from the pole! It was stuck! It wouldn't budge! The principal explained that they had used all the normal strategies to get her finger "unstuck" including trying vaseline jelly around it, and icing it to get the swelling down, etc., etc. to no avail! Now it was time for the rest of the school to start coming out for lunch recess break, but all the other students were forced to stay in their classrooms and eat lunches inside until they could get Allie's situation under control!

He thought that it probably would be wise if Nick or I could come by and help reassure Allie at this point. He also explained that he had called the Fire Department and the Santa Clara police, and they were coming to assess the situation! My principal heard my retelling of the story, and immediately sent someone to substitute in my Fifth grade classroom so that I could take off!

As I approached the school, I saw fire trucks and police cars on the Carden playground, surrounding my daughter. She was now wrapped in a fire proof heavy robe, which would prevent her from getting hit by sparks as they had to use a welder to cut the pole down! Then use a metal cutting tool to get as close as they could to the stuck finger! I showed up and raised my partially missing ring finger and said, "Hi! I'm the mom!" Allie was bravely weathering the storm, not crying, but looking rather freaked out! The firemen shook their heads in a little bit of dismay, and went back to the job at hand.

Now about this time, another fun adventure started. Apparently the local news stations get all the police reports in the area, and they had sent out a camera crew to film the event! Now I had to deal news people milling around, trying to get interviews with the staff and me as to what had occurred. This made me furious, and I tried to chase them off, but they got their way and just kept filming and interviewing.

They sure enough had Allie and the finger in the pole story as a featured segment of the San Jose nightly news! Why or why do we have so many finger troubles in our family, I'll never know!

Anyway, after that, all the Santa Clara Unified Schools had to get all their basketball and volleyball poles inspected and all the holes covered up! So I guess she did the community a service!

Visiting Mom

I wrote this memory on April, 2, 2002

I remember making all kinds of excuses why I couldn't go yet... there is a huge pile of laundry in the garage, the shaggy dog licking my face needs a bath, someone needs to start dinner, on and on. Weekends are always packed tight for us. So it was easy to make up those multiple excuses.

While the reasons I couldn't go yet were playing loudly over and over in my mind, I was feeling so burdened with guilt, I knew that even driving to see Mom would be incredibly painful. My feet would seem to drag as if formed of cement as I trudged down the path from my house to the car to set off on this journey. Just the actual physical movements of putting the key into the ignition to start the car into gear would seem to move in slow motion.

Never could I allow myself to remember the times when we disagreed or fought. These thoughts would bring back too many painful memories. As much as I yearned to remember the days gone past when Mom could be her old vibrant, energetic self, those were times we would never experience again. I had to admit I would never experience my "real Mom" again. In her place now was another person, another somebody, who was now a stranger to me, a mere skeleton of the person I once knew. Visiting Mom at her adult care home for dementia and Alzheimer's patients was so excruciatingly painful and full of sadness for me.

It was so vividly clear that I would never again know my mother as her self, but only this skeleton with a frail body, foggy mind, and an unwilling tongue, sitting before me, so unlike the person I yearned to know once again. The guilt is what would just devour me inside. She is my Mom, shouldn't I be overjoyed to see her? Shouldn't I be a big enough person to want to cradle her in my arms and show her my love? Why did my feet drag so heavily as I walked to the door? Why was the small talk with the caregivers always so difficult? If we could have had some privacy, maybe I might have felt less self-conscious.

Eventually, I was able to share with Grant, my big brother, all about the guilt I felt inside. His business schedule, gratefully, allowed him to begin to visit the Bay Area quite regularly. When he came to town, together we would make that drive to Mom's residence. The trip was now bearable for me. What a difference it made to have someone who understood the pain to make the journey with. I want to thank you, my brother Grant, for those final special days with our Mom.

Soccer Mom stories

When Nick, Josh, Caleb and I finally moved to Santa Clara in 1984, to our home on Fairlane Avenue, I knew we were in a permanent place where we could put down roots. I also knew that the boys needed to make new friends in the area, and what better way but to join a soccer team?

I was working full time as an engineering secretary at Failure Analysis Associates in Palo Alto, and getting the kids to soccer practice was going to be a challenge, but here goes! I contacted the Santa Clara soccer club and they said, "Sorry, all the teams are full unless you volunteer to coach a team!" So, with the help of Bill and his wife, neighbors around the corner, we managed to get a sketchy but workable plan together. I successfully negotiated with Bill, and he pretty much took over all the coaching!

Allie started playing soccer after Margaret W. invited her to join Bob J.'s co-ed team made up of her fellow kindergarteners at

Collins Elementary. She wasn't wild about the idea at first, and she loved these very unhealthy Squeeze-it juice drinks at the time, so I would bribe her with one every time she went to practice. Eventually they went on to be a premier soccer team for girls, and Allie stayed on Bob's team until high school. She juggled Youth group at church, being in San Jose Musical Theatre plays, soccer practice, Church choir practices, volleyball games through Carden del Encanto, and homework fairly well.

Several funny memories from those soccer days I will never forget. The times Nikki and Jeff would be playing somewhere at the soccer fields, and I would see Linda A. approaching, and I would immediately freak out and start asking everyone"Have you seen Jeff? Where's Jeff?" After babysitting for Linda so many years, I still felt accountable each time she came near! I lived in dreaded fear that I would lose him, rarely thinking of losing Nikki! Vinko used to tease me unmercifully about this!

Bob would print out these incredibly complicated MapQuest directions to all these various sites of soccer games all over the Silicon Valley area, and these were in the days ways before cell phones and Google Maps, so I would be frantically trying to interpret Allie's reading the directions to me while I raced down unfamiliar freeways and streets to get to games on time. Most of the parents on the soccer team drove with way more confidence and speeds that resembled "bats out of Hell" than I did, and I often thought part of their joint fun was to see how fast they could drive to try to trip me up and get me to miss an important turn. Trust me, that happened a lot!! Also, Linda was always calling at the last minute for me to pick up Julie to take her, because she had a conflict come up. I always felt driven to the point of exhaustion making all those soccer game trips! If I was smart, I'd bring the class and homework pages that I had to correct and get the teenagers on the soccer team to help me grade them when they had breaks between games. I think Allie one year had more games than 365 days in a year!

One time, we had games in San Diego or Los Angeles and all the team got completely covered in mud. We had to find laundromats between games to get them cleaned up, and then back to the motel for showers. I think one time we rented a motel just for the showers!

Another time, Allie couldn't find a bathroom and had to go in the woods on the side of the field. Not sure about all the funny details about that one!

I'll never forget the time I had to cut my way across the median strip on Highway 85 trying to get to one of Allie's volleyball games at some private Catholic School in South San Jose! The secretary at my school had taken a message in an undecipherable handwriting style for me on a little scrap of paper, and before

Google Maps and cell phones, I barely made it there in time!

I think I showed up more in my Jazzercise leotards to pick up Allie after soccer games than in regular clothes those days! She would always be rolling her eyes and acting like she wanted to die every time I showed up with a thong leotard on. Hey, I had to use my time wisely and I had to get my exercise too! But secretly I think I really did have a bit of fun trying to stir the pot a bit with that one!

Then Nikki started playing soccer too, so this meant we would be racing from one game to the next all weekend long. Add in her gymnastics meets, and Nick would take one kid, and and I would take the other, and we'd hit the road every weekend going to meets and games all over the state! By Sunday nights we would all fall into bed in exhaustion!

Ready to get up and start the whole thing over again on Monday mornings!

Rapid City, South Dakota Vacation

This happened when Allie was about nine, and Nikki about five. My friend Elaine, a fellow teacher at R. F. Kennedy School in the Franklin-McKinley District, and her husband Bob, owned a condo in Rapid City and asked to come visit them over the summer vacation.

We didn't have a very big car at this point, and we wanted to be comfortable driving all that ways. So we rented a big Lincoln Town car, and shoved all our camping gear, tents, sleeping bags, cooking stove, and pots and pans! Then we headed out, hoping to camp out part of the way to make it more of an adventure!

We drove through Reno, and up through Idaho, and cut across to South Dakota. I'll never forget what happened next! I remember it was a really hot day, and we had the windows down to keep the air circulating! Nikki and Allie were in the back seat, when all of a sudden we heard the sound of a great big hornet's nest coming from behind us on the highway! We jerked all of our heads around at the same time, and our eyes opened wide as saucers as I saw a swarm of motorcycles coming up on our left, and passing us as they flew by! Some of the women were sitting at the back of the motorcycle seats, holding on to their partners for dear life, and some were on their own bikes. Many were wearing skimpy bikini tops and short cut offs, distracting any one whom they passed by. Nick looked like he could barely keep his eyes on the road, and Nikki and Allie and I were laughing hysterically!

Well, so much for camping out! When we drove by the KOA campground that night to try to land a spot, the parking area looked like a Harley Davidson convention! All the bikers had completely taken over the place, and it was packed to the brim! We ended up calling Elaine to explain that we would be arriving a day early, due to the change in our camping schedule!

It ended up being a fantastic family vacation. I have told many people since then to try that part of the country for a great trip when your kids are in elementary school . They had wonderful walking mazes, the Crazy Horse Monument carved into the cliffside, water slide parks, Mt. Rushmore, and Black Hills, the town of Sturgis, and more!

Now it clicked why there were so many motorcycles! We had arrived the exact week of the Sturgis Harley festival! The girls' eyes were wide open again as we visited Sturgis, and they saw all the goings on! What an eye popping experience that was!

Camping with a Cinnamon Bear

This camping experience happened with Allie was about ten and Nikki was about seven, if my memory serves me well. We had loaded up one of our cars with a big trunk full of all our camping gear, tents, sleeping bags, camping stove, camping pots and pans, a coffee pot, some lake stuff, a propane lantern, flashlights, a cooler full of food, and even the kids' bikes strapped to the back of the car on a bike rack, and headed off to go camping near Reno. We ended up at a campground that was near a little lake where you could rent boats and such and other family oriented activities.

We were all settling in to set up our tent, and get all cozied up with the feel of the place, and getting all situated. Little kids were out riding bikes around the pathways that circled the campground, and there was a general feel of familial happy ambiance around the whole scene. All of a sudden out of the blue we heard a loud racket happening pretty close to our campsite!! It was a loud racket of pots and pans being banged together and spoons hitting pans, and people yelling and freaking out!! We all stopped right in our tracks and in unison looked over to see what was all the commotion about!!

A very large, golden brown adult cinnamon colored bear was standing on his hind legs, next to one of the family picnic tables, right in the campground! He was lifting up a gigantic gallon can of Cremora, and dumping it all over his face and upper body, lapping up the powdered creamy coffee creamer as fast as he could! It was the funniest sight! Soon he was partly covered white at the top of his chest and head, and the people all around were standing back trying to get him to leave by banging on their kitchen utensils and honking their car horns as loud as they could. He eventually got on all fours and proceeded to climb up a very tall Redwood tree which was in the middle of the campground! Then the racket really got up to a crescendo, with more and more people joining in the chorus to get him to go away! Finally after much ado, he came down and lumbered away, not fast or anything, just in his own good time, supposedly off to find the next goodie of the night.

We ended up staying at that campground that night, as far as I remember, figuring that he had already caused enough of a commotion in our neck of the woods, and was off to better hunting grounds.

The next day, clouds looked threatening and it looked like a storm was coming up. Now what you have to know about Nick is he is used to major creature comforts, and going camping is really a stretch for him, but he went along with the whole idea as long as the weather cooperated and the meals were tolerable. We were running out of good food, so I think the two girls and I went to the nearest town to get some groceries for dinner while Nick held the fort at the campsite. Basically anything less than beach weather was unacceptable to Nick as far as camping outside went.

When we were driving back from town, all set to cook dinner with the stuff we had purchased, we saw rain clouds near the camping area, and dark clouds gathering as we drove. When we got back to the campsite, Nick was fit to be tied. He was huddling inside the tent as the flaps and ropes tethering the tents down blew all around him, and he was furious! He said this was unacceptable and he wanted to leave now!!

We ended up loading everything in the pouring rain into the trunk of the car, got out of the campground as fast as we could, and ended up at a motel in South Lake Tahoe for the night. We got some quick dinner at a crummy restaurant near the motel, and called it a night.

Somewhere in this story I remember something about the girls discovering a rated R movie channel that we never found out about until much later!! Kids, you are welcome to correct any details in this story, but I told it with the best accuracy that I could muster this many years later!

Cream Soda Camping

This camping adventure happened at Fallen Leaf Campground, near Lake Tahoe. Allie must have been about thirteen, and Nikki about nine. Nikki brought along her best friend and partner in crime, Michelle, on this trip. We had two different tents by this time, because we couldn't all squish into one backpacking tent any more!

We spent the days at Fallen Leaf Lake floating in the waves, taking walks around the trails surrounding the lake, and even renting horses and horsey back riding! We may have even brought along bikes and hooked them to the bike rack at the back of the car. I remember lots of trips taking lots of long bike rides all throughout the forests surrounding Fallen Leaf Lake and Lake Tahoe.

Evenings were spent around a campfire, cooking dinner on a cook stove, and roasting marshmallows. The bathrooms had showers so we could clean ourselves up, and the girls all pitched in washing dishes at the sink near the bathrooms. Then we would pile all the cooking gear and food and coolers into the trunk of our car at night, and try to erase any sign of cooking from our campsite. The garbage cans were all equipped with a hook, where you had to manually attach one metal part to another, to help keep the bears from breaking in the dumpsters at night. Still, you were pretty much dependent upon the other campers in near proximity to you to follow the housekeeping rules for food. If they didn't, the bears were smart enough to come around scavenging for left over goodies each night. Also, we went to sleep each night hearing loud cries of coyotes off in the distance. EWWWWWW!

One night, we heard a deep sniffing sound right around our campsite. You seriously could not ignore this loud sniffing sound! Pretty obvious it was a bear, or maybe two! Just think of how big their nasal snouts are, and you can imagine how loud the sniffing sound was! We all just shivered in our sleeping bags, and eventually they went away! You never dared get up in the middle of the night to go to the restroom! Way too scary!

When we woke up the next morning, super early, we heard loud yelling coming from the neighbor's campsite. Apparently, one of the campers was sleeping underneath the picnic table, and someone else in their group had left a whole box of donuts out on the table all night long! When Mr. Bear smelled the donuts, he obviously started in on a munch feast, waking up the unsuspecting camper from his deep slumber! That's when the loud banging noises started, as he escaped for his dear life, and alerted his family to help him!

As we finally stopped watching with absolute shock at the scene going on in the campground right near us, we saw huge, dusty paw prints on the back of the car trunk where all of our food was stored. Fortunately for us, he did not try to break into the windows or trunk, or doors to sniff around and get some more to eat! We also noticed on the side of our campground a crinkled up aluminum can of cream soda. Oh Oh! That was our mistake! We had some soda pop the night before, and apparently one can had gone unnoticed when we packed up the food for the night. It looked like the bear had just scrunched up the can with his claws, all the while drinking up the creamy syrupy liquid!

We kept that scrunched up can on a shelf in our family room for quite a long time, as a momento of our scary night of camping! And lots more story telling when guests would notice it and ask why it was displayed on our shelf!

First Trip to Venice

This memory is from the year of around 1998, when Allie was about twelve and Nikki was about nine years old. Nick's mom, Barbara, had recently lost her husband and Nick's father, Marsh, after a long illness, and she was feeling nostalgic about some of the trips they had taken over the years of their long marriage. It was just about Christmas time, and she called and insisted that she wanted us to take a trip to Venice, that she would pay for our expenses! But the offer only would stand if we could go as soon as possible! She was strange that way, and we knew she meant it. She would renege on her promise if we dilly dallied around, so we said we would try as best we could to go before Christmas!

Nick and I had never traveled to Italy before, and so of course we consulted our most experienced traveler in the family, United pilot Uncle Jimbo, and he recommended that Venice in the Christmas season would be just grand! We started making babysitting arrangements for the two girls, and found friends who were willing to take them for the time that we would be gone. Travel arrangements were moving ahead smoothly, when Nick mentioned the trip to some of the people he worked with, and one gave him a huge discounted coupon for the Gritti Palace, one of the premier hotels in the city. Uncle Jimbo offered some buddy passes on United Airlines to the two of us, and we made our reservations leaving from San Francisco, transferring in Washington D. C. and arriving at the Milan airport, where we would then take a train to Venice!

We were all set! Now the only thing left to do was pack and lock up the house. I checked the weather in Venice in December and it did not look favorable! Freezing cold temperatures were the norm, and heavy clothes would be essential. We needed heavy sweaters, hats, gloves, parkas, heavy boots, and the like. Aha! I had just finished knitting a beautiful Icelandic Lopi wool black and white sweater and matching hat, which I was intending to give to my niece Julie, who lived in Maine. It would be the perfect wardrobe addition to my travel bag! I figured I could hand wash it and make it just like new again once I got back. She knew I was knitting it for her as I had shared several times the progress I was making on her gift. She couldn't wait until it was all done!

Off we went to the airport, only to find out that our tickets were only secure on a standby basis through to the first leg of the trip. But we were nestled next to each other in our seats as the flight set off to fly out of San Francisco. But , then our first surprise occurred! The pilot came on the loud speaker and informed us that there were mechanical difficulties on the plane, and we would be returning to SFO. We never even got off the ground!

Then, as we scurried about the San Francisco airport, Nick and I got separated, but he was able to secure a flight right away to London. I was left in San Francisco, trying to get any flight on its way towards Europe. I ended up getting on a United flight to Washington, D. C. Nick ended up spending two days in London, trying to get a flight to Milan! I was able to get as far as Washington, D. C. Once I arrived I would again have to wait and be put on another standby list, and I had to wait all day and night in Washington, D.C. alone, while Nick went off to Milan!

I booked a hotel room in Washington, D. C. for the night, and decided to play tourist in the capital all day while I had to wait. I had never seen the Lincoln Memorial, or visited any of the other sights in the city before, as it was my first time there too! After a glorious day of seeing the various landmarks, I set my alarm for early the next day, and got to the airport in time to catch my standby flight. I was finally on my way to Italy! Of course, all this was before we had cell phones, and Nick and I had no way of communicating once he went off to London alone. We ended up spending two whole days separated at the very beginning of our romantic get away trip!

We both eventually made it to Milan just fine, not on the same flights, of course, and made my way to the baggage claim area to pick up my bag, which had all my week's clothes in it, along with the handmade sweater and hat. As luck would have it, the bag was missing. Apparently because I was flying standby, my bag did not make it on the flight with me, and it would have to be delivered to my hotel by the airlines. I gave them the name of the Gritti Hotel, hoping with all of my might that it would arrive safely!! The only thing I was thinking was how horrible it would be if I had to start all over again on the sweater and hat ensemble; I think I must have worked on it for several months!

This is a funny part of the story! I made it to the Milan train station from the airport, and was trying with all my might to read the huge screen with all the various train schedules flashing, constantly changing every twenty seconds or so. As I was gazing so intently on the screen, I mistakenly stepped in a huge pile of dog poop! People in Europe travel freely with their pets everywhere. I guess some body did not notice that their dog had pooped, and had just left it there as they rushed off to their train! Here I was, completely unaware of my predicament, when all of a sudden a group of travelers around me started pointing down at my shoe and snickering! My shoe was covered quite a bit with the offending mess, and I had no idea what to do! I searched for paper towels or a Kleenex box, anything, but ended up having to walk quite a ways through the station to get to the women's restroom! After cleaning it off the best I could, I was back to the huge screen to try to find a train to Venice. What a way to start my time in glorious Italy!

After managing to catch the right train to Venice, I now had to get on the correct Vaporetto to take me to the Santa Marta del Giglio stop nearest to the hotel! Still unable to contact Nick in any way, I just meandered down the narrow, winding passageways in this incredible, ancient city to eventually find my way to the Gritti Palace!

Of course, he wasn't just waiting around for me to arrive, so I had to check in with the concierge and let them know I had arrived to meet up with my husband! This hotel was just the most elegant place I had ever seen! It had been recently restored (to the tune of $60 million) to its original splendor, and it was the home of a former Venetian doge, Andrea Gritti, a true noble's residence, with a terrace that nearly faces St Mark's Basilica and the Campanile, the bell tower. When the sun bathes it in golden light in the evenings as it is going down, you feel like you're immersed in glamour. It was definitely radiating romance and elitism, and there were photos of Peggy Guggenheim, Ernest Hemingway, Elizabeth Taylor and Richard Burton as former guests decorating various walls. Obviously, feeling completely out of place, I just settled down in the bar area, ordered a stiff drink, and tried to regroup the best I could, knowing no Italian at all, and jet lagged to boot!

We eventually met up, and walked, and dined, and shopped, and went sightseeing until exhaustion, and my suitcase still had not shown up. After three days, I was gloriously greeted by the concierge's message that my suitcase had been found and was on it's way! The best part of all was I didn't have to spend three more months knitting! After about eight days of glorious romance and intrigue, we were on our way back home! And this time we got to travel all the way back home together!

Teachers' Trip to China

Erin L. was a second grade teacher at Bishop Elementary one year, it was the year before the Beijing Olympics, around 2007. The teachers used to gather around the staff room tables each day to share stories of our lives as we ate our sack lunches. One day Erin was talking about how she really wanted to go to China, and since she was a fluent Mandarin speaker, she could be a suitable tour guide and trip arranger! So she inquired if any of us would be interested. And so, lo and behold, that July six of us were off to Mainland China! The group included her niece, in junior high, Cindy, Cindy's sister Denice, Nicole, Erin, and myself!

Our first destination was Beijing, where Erin knew some friends who ended up helping out taking care of some of our excess luggage, as we took car tours, van excursions, and train rides all around the nation. I remember riding in a three wheeled bicycle with the driver steering us in the front, racing across busy city streets against traffic, while we held on for dear life! Racing down alleys and yelling out hello in Chinese which sounded like "Me Yeow" in English!

Once, when we were loading up in our three wheeler bicycle, and Cindy and Erin's niece were nestled in the back, and the driver got off the seat for a moment. They tipped over backwards, with the bike all toppled over, and their feet stuck high up in the air, and they bumped their heads as they fell! The Chinese in the neighborhood who saw it were hysterical in laughter, as they watched us all try to bring the bicycle back into an upright position! They ran into their houses to get their cameras so they could record it on film!

Erin's Mandarin Chinese skills came in handy when we would check into a hotel, and they tried to give us a higher price on the room than was standard. But because she could understand what they were saying, she could catch them in the act of trying to rip us off!

One morning, it was the crack of daylight, and everyone else was fast asleep. I saw all kinds of commotion going on outside my window, so I got dressed and went out to see what was it all about. They were having a sidewalk Flea Market/Farmer's Market. I saw a cute dress and a top that I liked, and the prices were phenomenally low, so I tried to size them up and decided a large would fit! (The sizes for things were abnormally on the small size!) I raced back to the room with my purchases, and put on the dress. It fit so well, I thought I better go down and buy another one. When the Chinese saw the "haole" in that dress, a whole crowd of them swarmed up to the table to buy one like mine! I ended up with only one dress! When I got back to the hotel, everyone was surprised to see that I was wearing my new pretty dress, as they were just rubbing the sleep out of their eyes!

Whenever we went out to a restaurant for a meal, we would all just trust Erin to order food that would be palatable and tasty. Sometimes we never really knew what we were eating! And if one of us would come down with any kind of digestive problem, we would head out to a McDonald's, order the same kind of food we got in the States, and our tummies would immediately be rid of all their troubles!

The funniest thing that happened was on the Wild Wall of the Great Wall of China. We had already visited the Golden Wall, and now we hired a private van to take us to a more rugged part of the Wall! As we approached our drop off spot, the road became harder to navigate, and muddier, and more slippery as we went up the hill! Eventually, we had to literally get out of the van and help the driver and his assistant push it out of the muddy road, and back to business again! We tried to keep clean as we could, but at this rate, we were doomed to be messy! Little did we know what muddy trails awaited us as we began to trudge up the mountain paths behind our guides! We ended up seeing quite a bit more than we bargained for, and on the way back some of us were slipping so much we literally had to get down and slide down some of the pathways on our butts! Some Chinese workmen were working in the area that day, and I will never forget their faces when they saw this group of "haole" American tourists coming down with our muddy clothes! They couldn't help but laugh right in front of us! Some of us had to just ditch these clothes in the dumpster when we got back to the hotel that day!

We eventually took a train ride across the Mainland to Xian, in the Shaaxi, area of China, so we could visit the Terracotta Army Cultural Museum. We stayed in Xian for several days, and while we were there we discovered a great massage center within walking distance from our hotel. We showed up in the evening after a day of sightseeing, and were welcomed in the lobby. Then escorted to a dressing room where we were to dress up in little gowns, and then taken to a huge room covered with lounges, where our massages would all happen as we laid next to each other in this large darkened room! After we were all settled into our lounges ready for our massages to begin, a group of about six young men came out, all dressed in nylon basketball outfits! These were our massage therapists for the night! They did excellent work, and made all our sore muscles disappear! I'll never forget how weird it all was, and the worst part of all was we had to walk by all these little side businesses on the way back of young women selling their "wares" in the Xian red light district! That was where out hotel was in proximity!

Many other funny stories happened on this trip. I was always wearing makeup and trying the best I could to fix my hair, using foam rollers at night and gel to get some curl in my hair. When we would go to check out of our hotels, they would look meticulously at all our bed linens and towels, and if they thought there were too many makeup marks on them, we would have to pay an additional cleaning charge! After a few times of getting nabbed with these charges, I figured out how to be a bit neater when it came to taking care of my grooming troubles! I would stay back and let Erin try to explain away the situation, all the while croaking in my boots that I would be embarrassed again! And all the rest of my travel mates would be rolling their eyes at me, once again!

More Teaching Wardrobe Failures

The first one happened at R. F. Kennedy School and I was teaching Fifth Grade. We were given huge amounts of freedom as to which methods we used to reach our students. We had programs like a Describimento Science program that Dr. Charles Parchment introduced to our district to combine bilingual Spanish and English lessons with Science and Art. This was right up my alley, so I spent many hours at the Franklin McKinley District office going through the various lessons and bins and carting the materials back to my classroom. Kids could work in small groups on hands on experiments to come up with their own hypotheses about what they were studying.

These ready made lessons were so successful and popular with my students that I self created "stations" for Social Studies and Science on other topics, where students would work in a small group of about 4-5 students, and would rotate through the various activities over about a three week rotation schedule. Each group had a symbol, and I had created a whole system of how they would move through these over the course of study. I created map activities, interactive reading lessons, game boards with questions from our Social studies books, vocabulary match up activities, puzzles to put together with the facts from our lessons, and others. It took hours and hours to develop these, and most of this development had to happen at home in the evenings or weekends. One time I was invited to share these at an Asilomar reading conference outside of Carmel, CA.

The one real drawback was it took at least twenty to thirty minutes in the middle of the school day to get these seven stations all set up. I figured out that the best set up time was my lunch period, so I mostly skipped lunch with my peers, and spent the lunch hours on Mondays through Thursdays setting up my "stations".

This is where the story gets funny. I would be dashing around my classroom, all alone, snacking on a sandwich and a bottle of water, and then racing to go to the restroom before the kids came back. All the groups would be completely set up for the next forty-five minutes of learning. On this particular day, I went to go get my students from the line on the blacktop, and led them back to the classroom, with me at the head of the line. As soon as we got to the classroom door, the girl who had been at the front of the line tugged hard on my floor length skirt. The skirt had been tucked into the back of my panty girdle, and I had been "traipsing" down the full length of the hallways like that, with my panty girdle showing for all my students and fellow teachers to see! Luckily, no one ever said anything, so maybe she was my savior that day!

Another giant wardrobe failure happened when I taught a Fourth and Fifth grade combination class at Fairwood Elementary in Sunnyvale. Once again, I was trying to make the Social Studies curriculum more hands-on and intriguing for my students, so we were making salt and dough maps. The Fifth graders were creating salt dough maps of the United States, and the Fourth graders were making maps of California. They had to use their fingers to shape the dough on a piece of heavy cardboard, and using a real map as a guide, add in all the topographical features by shaping mountains, rivers, valleys, and hillsides.

The day finally came when all the maps were created and dry enough to paint, so we mixed up all the tempura paint colors in separate cups and were going to finish up outside. Green was for the coastal regions, light beige for the deserts, blue for the rivers and oceans, gold for the hillsides, orange for the higher hills, and red for the steepest mountains, just like you would see on a real topographical map.

I always encouraged the kids to help me when we had to cart things outdoors, so on this particular occasion one of my students was carrying a large container of bright red paint. I bet you can guess what happened!! Sure enough, he tripped as he was walking and the entire contents of the paint went flying across the air, landing square on the long floral dress I was wearing that day! Imagine the look of shock on both of our faces as we stared down at the drippy, sloppy, oozing paint glob which was now rushing towards the ground.

I just went in the room, scraped off the paint that I could, mixed up another batch of red, went back outside and kept directing the lesson, and that was that! By the end of the day, the paint had dried and was chipping off in large chunks. I had a teacher training to attend after school that day, so what do you think I did? I just went to the training the way I was, and luckily my dress's original color was mostly red floral, so not that many people noticed.

From that day on, I always had an extra outfit and extra shoes in my classroom, and an extra coat and sweater too for cold days. One of the best lessons I ever taught my fellow teachers was to always have a back up outfit. You never knew when you might need one!

As the years went on, and I had to go to yoga at 6AM and head back to school and change in my classroom, I added in a whole "Beauty salon" of makeup, lotions, perfume, a curling iron, and hair brushes to my closet! And always a two pound box of See's Candy as a daily reward of one piece after I said goodbye to the kids each afternoon! Hey, teachers work hard and we have to take care of ourselves!

Thailand with Josh

This happened when Josh was living in Bangkok, I think in 2009, and working as a teacher in elementary, high school, and colleges! He had recently completed his Master's degree in Education, and decided he was up for an adventure! I had some free time, so he invited me to come for a ten day visit.

I made a lot of mistakes on this trip, as usual. First of all, it's probably best to just grab a taxi from the airport to get to your hotel, rather than pre booking one through a website to pick you up from your flight. I had already paid for my pre booked taxi, and yet when he dropped me off he wanted me to pay in Thai cash! I didn't even have any with me yet, so we had to go to a street side ATM and get some, which probably was not a very secure idea. I ended up paying twice for one taxi ride! This happened within the first hour of my visit, which did not increase my traveling confidence!

Once I reached my hotel, I realized there was a safe, and proceeded to put my valuables in it. However, later in the week I discovered that one of the hotel staff was able to jerry-rig it, and some of my US cash had disappeared, along with more Thai money. Those were both disheartening experiences, and since the hotel concierge feigned ignorance about the theft, I was just left holding the bag! More adventures surely to come! Luckily, I still had my passport!

Josh had to work quite a bit during the week, so we took only a couple of days for a side trip to an exotic island called Koh Samed, a ferry ride away from the coast of Thailand. The sad part of that trip was as we were headed out on a Friday night from Bangkok, we kept stopping to pick up attractively dressed young women to join our van. I realized later that they were working as "paid escorts" in the holiday town for the weekend, and when Sunday evening came around, other young women were headed back to Bangkok with us again! I found this really disheartening and sad!

I found out that as long as you could prove that you had a steady source of income, and you did not have to work in Thailand as a foreigner in order to live there, the Thai government would welcome you with open arms to live there. People could live on a very limited amount of money in Thailand as far as US standards go, with a house on the white sand beaches, and a maid and a cook to boot! However, the language barriers are rather great, as their alphabet does not even come close to resembling ours. I found the language difficulties to be rather great, much greater than traveling in Europe.

So far, it sounds like my visit there was not very positive! But that is not really the case. I am just remembering some of the ways that this trip was more challenging than any other I had ever taken before.

Now came my biggest adventure of all! Josh thought I would enjoy going on a solo visit to Chiang Mai, in the north western corner of the country. I booked a tour through a tourist office in Bangkok, which necessitated a train ride at night from Bangkok to Chiang Mai. I had taken other train rides in China, so I thought it sounded pretty doable! All was fine on the train until early morning came, and I woke up with the birds and everyone else on the train was sound asleep. I had some instant coffee packets and freeze dried noodle cups in my backpack, so I found the hot water dispenser near the restroom, and helped myself to a styrofoam cup and some hot water for a soothing cup of coffee, while I rested against my pillow and read.

When the rest of the passengers were starting to wake up, the train stopped and the wait staff for our car of the train came on to serve us treats and beverages for a cost. The lady in charge of serving our car was furious with me! How had I had the audacity to help myself to her water and cup without paying!! Once again, my previous travel experiences in China did not match up with Thailand rules! In China, the water and cups were available at all hours for no charge, but this was not the case in Thailand. She was so mad I thought I was going to be arrested for theft, and thrown off the train! Fortunately, for me, there was another very kind Samaritan on the train who spoke fluent English who helped explain to her that I thought the water and cups were for free, just like I had in China, and I was more than happy to pay her now! I offered an amount of money way over the charge she would require, but the furious woman would not take my money, as if it was below her to accept it now!

When I exited the train, I sheepishly looked about for Thai police officers, who I thought might have been alerted to my thieving ways, and would be laying in wait to arrest me! But, luckily, my tour guide was there to gather me right up, and loaded us into his open back truck to get on to our next adventure. We all sat at the back of his truck, on little benches, loaded our backpacks in at our feet, and proceeded to take off down the busy highways of rural Thailand to the mountainous area where we were going to backpack up to the pretty hillsides, and stay a few nights! I had survived another close call!

Here's where another scary part of my adventure began! We had guides leading us up a steep mountain trail, but the problem was that I was the only fluent English speaker, and most of the other foreigners were French tourists. I started huffing and puffing as we went higher and higher, and the smoke in the air became thicker and thicker from nearby fires in the area. My asthma really started acting up, and I had to stop quite often to catch my breath and use my inhaler, which luckily I had along with me! After a while, our guides took turns carrying my backpack so that I would have an easier time traveling! This was my first experience of feeling old, as I was the "most mature" one in the group! Finally, we made it to our mountain encampment, and I could catch my breath again! I remember taking dips in mountain lakes, and yummy Thai cooking, and all of us pitching in to do general housekeeping tasks like washing dishes and sweeping our tent floors. We also took a water raft ride down a wild Thai river, and rode elephants as part of our adventure!

Thank goodness, this time I had a cell phone! It was so cold at night, I remember shivering in my bed clothes, and listening to pod casts on my phone in the middle of the night when I was so cold I couldn't sleep! I was thankful when I arrived back at my Bangkok Hotel after such an exciting solo trip!

The street markets in Bangkok were festive and crowded and full of delightful aromas of street food. We could get a huge bowl of noodles, vegetables, and meat for around $1.00! Traveling in Thailand was extremely affordable. Once again, when Josh was working, I would flag down a three wheeler and scoot about town, visiting temples and other sights. I remember one day they were having a political protest march and lots of lots of noise and commotion in the streets. I was wearing a bright red skirt that day, and I noticed that one of the colors of the marching crowds was red! I kept hoping that no one would be upset with me wearing the color of the other side! Whew! Made it through that adventure too!

All in all, I would recommend traveling to these exotic locations in a group rather than going on a solo trip! I think, just maybe, you figured that bit of advice out for yourself after reading this!

So Many Business Ideas!

I guess I've always had more energy than normal, so even though I have been working most of my life in a regular job, I have always found ways to make money on the side with little crazy business ideas! I still have several hobbies to this day, and an Etsy store to prove this!

Even when I was only 20 years old, and living in Santa Rosa up on the road to Calistoga, I had an Aunt Mary's Apple Butter business! It was just a silly way to fill up time, but I've always been drawn to having a little business going in my life.

When we lived on the ranch in Stevensville, Montana, I would wake up early Saturday mornings, with my car all filled with farm produce, and would sell at the Missoula Farmer's Market.

When we lived in Missoula, I hounded my neighbors leaving Avon catalogs on their doorsteps. I wanted to win a contest one time, so I discounted all the perfume prices, and ended up

winning the silly nightgown and robe ensemble contest!
I also went on to try my hand at Mary Kay Cosmetics. I even made it to the Director in Qualification level, before my life fell apart during my divorce and that business went away by the way side when I moved to CA.

When Nikki and Allie were in non-stop soccer practices, play practices, and gymnastics classes, and dance classes, I would take along my papers to grade and my knitting. I always made good use of my time, even knitting hats at stoplights! Nikki would watch for the green light, I would knit at the red lights, and then she'd yell out " Green, Mom!" and I'd go again. I used to say I could knit a hat a week at the stop lights I drove those kids around so much!

That brings me to the Book Business! Oh boy, this was a killer! I had this book scanner gizmo that I could take to any book sale or garage sale, and it would scan the barcode on the book and tell me what it was worth on Amazon. I must have had bookcases in every bedroom, nook and cranny of the garage, and under every bed in the house! The business got so busy that every day after school I would check my orders, have to race home after teaching all day, get the kids to soccer and dance class, then race to the post office to mail the books! It was the sound of the tape gun that drove every one absolutely crazy. To this day, my kids cannot wrap up a package with clear tape without thinking of the book business! I would sneak into the garage and try to use the tape gun as quietly as I could, and still somebody would always be woken up by that irritating noise! Nick was elated the day I decided to give the books that I had left to the Goodwill. He had to make multiple trips to get them all delivered.

When it was 2007, I took a pottery class at the Santa Clara Recreation Center, and by September of that year, I had convinced my principal at Fairwood to let me have the school kiln at home so that I could fire the students' projects. She didn't want the liability of my firing clay at school, so she agreed. So that started my pottery business! I got a wheel, and a bunch of glazes, and with my kiln I was ready to roll! I still have an Etsy store called MerryPotsandKnits where I sell my pottery, sewing, knitting, and wool felting projects. I just fired two loads of clay this week! I've participated in sales with my Orchard Valley Ceramics Arts Guild, and HupUp, a new way to sell, where you set up your table in front of a storefront for a day and pay them $20 to sell for one day. Those are always a lot of fun, but mostly I just love visiting with people about the stuff I make.

The funniest one of all was the scrunchie business. We went on a trip to Kona, and I saw a man making Hawaiian print scrunchies. I bought a few, disassembled them when I got home to see how he constructed them, and sure enough! There started the scrunchie business. I figured I could sell them to all the little gymnasts in Nikki's gymnastic classes. I got the California Sports Center to display them in their cabinet for a while, but as usual, it was an idea with a great plan, just not so much! The funny thing

is that Kaitlyn Bristowe, one of our favorite Bachelorettes, actually did start a successful scrunchie business, which Nikki loves to remind me of!

My kids cringe when they tell me that they are thinking that they need a little extra money. That gets my wheels turning and I always have to bite my tongue as I think for them and all the business ideas for them I just would love to be able to share! But in my old age, I've learned to "Wear beige and keep my mouth shut" unless someone asks for advice! I think just maybe I had to learn that the hard way........

Pumpkin Bites, Granola Bars, and a Can of Peanuts

This memory is from my 27th year of teaching elementary school. Once again, my classroom was located in a run down portable, filled with invisible holes in the walls, insect tracks hidden behind colorful bulletin boards, poor lighting, and located at the end of a whole line of other portable buildings in definite need of tearing down. Plans were being made to tear down this historic Sunnyvale school, which had been a landmark example for other elementary schools all of the state of California in the early 1950's.

Apparently this school was so highly regarded when it was brand new that bus loads of principals and superintendents from all over the state had visited this school as a prime example of the current state of the art construction and architectural design in the 1950's. The land had been donated to the city of Sunnyvale by the family of Jarvis E. Bishop, who had been the first

California serviceman to die in WWII. The grounds were laid out beautifully, with gardens of flowers and huge stately trees interspersed between buildings. The regular classrooms were far reaching and tall, with huge windows on one whole length of the classroom, and huge amounts of storage space.

Almost all of the teachers in the main classrooms were thrilled with their spacious rooms, even though they were now over 60 years old! But, now technology concerns, and keeping up with modern building codes, and aging plumbing was forcing the old buildings into being replaced by a new, high-tech, state of the art campus. It was just a matter of time before I would be moving out of this old decrepit portable into a spanking new 21st Century classroom.

It was near Halloween time when this story occurred. In years past, I had purchased six large pumpkins, and invited parents to volunteer to help small groups of students to cut open, design faces, and raffle off a pumpkin to one kid in each group to take home as part of our Halloween festivities. This year, I decided it would be fun to have each student bring in a smaller individual pumpkin, and we would decorate them with permanent Sharpie pens, glitter, and other decorations like little hats, jewels, and the like. Students starting bringing in their pumpkins, and we lined them up on the back table, getting ready for our celebratory decorating the day before Halloween.

At the same time, I was practicing yoga before school at a studio close by, and would race back to my classroom in the morning, change my clothes, put on some makeup, and eat a little breakfast before the students arrived. I generally kept snacks like high energy bars, granola bars, and cans of mixed nuts within close proximity to my classroom door, so that whenever I was hungry I could grab one as I raced outside to yard duty or to the office to make copies before class started.

During the week before Halloween, I entered the room and was shocked to find a half eaten granola bar on the table near the door, and another granola bar wrapper left empty on the floor! My first reaction was total confusion, and wonder about what could possibly have happened! It seemed so strange to think that someone might have been in the room over the night eating my granola bars! I had a wonderful relationship with the night custodian, and it seemed totally out of character for him to be eating my snacks!!

As I proceeded to get ready for the day ahead, I saw other strange evidences of something out of whack! Little bites were showing on the mini pumpkins! A can of mixed nuts had the plastic lid half chewed off, and most of the contents gone! AHA! Finally a light went on and I realized that my classroom had been the victim of a rat, or more than one rat!!

I raced to the office with a half eaten granola bar and the empty wrapper in my hands to show the main secretary the evidence. She promised that she would let the operations department at the district office know! And sure enough, later that day they were outside my room installing rat traps or poison under the portable, away from anyplace the students would be able to get into it.

I made it a practice to stand outside my classroom in the afternoon after school was dismissed to visit with the parents and make sure that all my students were picked up on time. There was a little area by some shady trees where toddlers and mothers would gather as they waited for students to be dismissed. After a day or so after the poison was put out, lo and behold, a huge mother rat with a big bulging tummy was dragging herself across the ground, moving very, very slowly and acting like she had been drugged! Now the evidence was right before our eyes! She eventually crawled back under the building, and I think we can presume that she was the culprit who was eating the goods! After that day, I never had any more bites taken out of my snacks, as I kept them in a metal locked file cabinet where no creature could get in! Ah! The adventures of teaching once again! Never a dull moment! Below is a picture of two of my best friend teachers and myself on Halloween in front of my infamous portable! My one friend is a friendly witch, I'm in the middle as Fern, and my other friend on the right is dressed as Wilbur the pig from the story Charlotte's Web!

A Kowloon Night Adventure

This happened when Nick was working at Loral Space Systems as a business and contracts negotiator. He had to work in Hong Kong for about a week, and they were putting him and his co-workers up at the Fairmont Hotel. So we discussed it and decided it would be fun for me to come along too!

He had to work long hours every day, Monday through Friday, with very few breaks. Finally, after working all day long even on Saturday, he got a night off! I had been bee- bopping all around Hong Kong and Kowloon all week, even taking a trip to Macau by myself. I had taken city buses, and hydroplane boat rides, and ferries all over the area, and had so many adventures. I couldn't wait to show Nick some of them!

All throughout the work week, I had become familiarized with museums, pretty parks, shopping areas, Buddhist temples where you could get your fortune read, yummy restaurants, The Bird Market, fancy hotels, and other sight seeing delights! I'd taken up the habit of just jumping on a bus that was heading down the main Kowloon street, and jumping off at various stops when I saw something of interest. So that is what I planned to do with Nick to show him some of the sights!

We headed out at dark, on our way down Kowloon town, and jumped on a bus. We were just chatting away and I was pointing out different sights to him, when all of a sudden we realized that this bus was not ever making any stops! As a matter of fact, we were now approaching a huge bridge, which spanned its way across a huge river and bay! I realized that this was not the sort of bus ride that we needed for a pleasant sightseeing trip!

I jumped up in horror, and went up to try to talk to the bus driver, who immediately tried to shoo me away, telling me "No talk! When driving bus!" Luckily for us, there was a very kind woman on the bus sitting near us who spoke fluent English. She could see the panic in my eyes, and asked if she could be of assistance! As I explained to her our predicament - out sightseeing, no passports with us, just out for a fun night on the town in Kowloon! Just then she explained that this was the nonstop, express bus to the inland of Communist China! You probably can imagine how absolutely infuriated Nick was at this point, traveling with his own Lucy Ricardo as a travel guide!

(What's funny is that Lucille Ball's daughter, Lucy Arnaz, and I were born only one week apart, in July, 1951!)

This kind Chinese woman was our lifesaver! She then went up and explained to the bus driver, and was able to convince him to take a side trip to a local bus terminal that was nearby our current location! He did just that, and you cannot believe the relief I felt as the bus came to an abrupt stop!

This Good Samaritan literally got off the bus with us, on a dark Saturday night, when she could have been going home to her family after a long work week. She walked with us several streets away, and pointed out the bus to get on that would take us back to the Fairmont Hotel! Can you imagine the hot water I might have been in had she not come to our aid? No passports, Nick stuck in Communist China, and not able to work? I hate to even think about it!

Miracles

These three miracles happened somewhere during the years of 2009-2011. This was during a period of my life where I was searching for God with my whole being, heart, soul, and body. I was praying for many hours a day, seeking the Lord in prayer, praying in my prayer language to the Holy Spirit, participating in Bible studies, teaching a Bible Club for the students of Bishop Elementary School in Sunnyvale, and attending many different gatherings of Christians in the Bay Area.

All throughout the day, while doing my daily tasks, I would be focused on seeing God where ever I was. If I was standing in a post office line, I would be praying for the strangers around me, while walking down sidewalks, I would be praying for the people in the houses, and while I was working in my gardens, I would be praying. This period in my life was an intense "God" time, unlike any other in my walk except for the first "honeymoon" period when I had just heard the call on my life, and gave my heart to Jesus when I accepted the Good News of forgiveness for my sins in my sophomore year of college.

I cannot really explain why this period of time occurred in my life, as my life has now returned to a much more "normal" pace. All I know is that I saw miracles happen to people I knew and to myself during this time. The three that I will share are just the most dramatic and most notable, but this is not meant to negate the other God moments I had during this time of my life.

Miracle #1 - The Wedding Ring

This happened on an Easter morning many years ago. I woke up early, like I often do, and had a deep desire to spend some quiet time with Jesus before church. I went on about a 2 1/2 mile walk all throughout my neighborhood, where I have been known to walk a common established route. And throughout the walk, I was praying and singing and listening to gospel music, and completely happy,, knowing I was close to God. I came home and got ready for church the normal way and did not notice until my hands were raised over my hands in the middle of the church service that the 1.2 carat diamond in my wedding ring had disappeared! I was rather shocked, but just continued through the service without saying anything except to my husband. I just prayed that God would help me find it! I told my friends at church to please look on the carpets and let me know if they found it!

After I got home, I was really bummed, so I decided to retrace my steps all the way back through the miles that I had walked, praying and walking while all the time searching the ground for my diamond, but to no avail. I just went on with the Easter day, cooking and washing dishes, and every so often looking all over the carpets inside the house too, just hoping my some chance my diamond would appear. When I went to bed that night, just before I went to sleep, I confessed to God that this diamond ring being lost was ruining my peace and destroying my fellowship with him, and I confessed that it was taking up way too much of my attention. And then I just "gave the problem to him", and said I was done worrying about it. After all, it was just a ring, it was not as important as my dear husband, and certainly not worth getting all upset about. I said I could be happy with a fake cubic zirconium if need be, and went to sleep to forget about it.

The next morning was a regular school day, and as usual I needed to race to get ready and out the door on time. I said hi to the Lord as I woke up, and as soon as I realized I was awake, I felt a huge desire to go check the carpet right by my dresser. It was if I woke up and was driven by a motor to go check on this one part of the room. The diamond was right there on the carpet!!! I yelled out to my husband, "I found it!" To this day, neither he nor I have ever been able to figure out why we never saw it there after scouring the house the day before.....I have always wondered if an angel returned it in the middle of the night....

Miracle #2 - The coffee cup

This happened in my classroom in Room 14 at Bishop Elementary School. It happened right after, maybe a few months, after the diamond reappearing miracle. It was a Monday morning, maybe 9:00 AM when it began.

It was just a few days after a major vacation break, and I was really sleepy and feeling pretty unenergetic that day. It was on a Monday and I had Bible Club in that room right after school, so it was going to be a long day. I needed all the pep I could get!

I decided to make myself a cup of instant coffee, so I put the electric hot water heater on, which was in a far corner of my classroom, and went back to teaching. When the heater came to a boil, I picked up my coffee cup and realized it was not completely clean. So I poured some of the boiling hot water into it, all the way to the top, and some liquid soap so that it would get sparkly clean. Just then one of my students came up and asked me a quick question, and because I was in a hurry to get back to teaching, I mistakenly put my hand into the cup to wash it out. I had my hand in boiling hot water!! Many years ago, I had a finger accident and I have to wear my wedding ring on my right hand. So my right hand was completely, hot, and I put it immediately into cold water at the sink to try to cool it off! I realized the danger I had created for myself, and under my breath, I said a quick prayer,"Please, Jesus, help me! Don't let this be a bad burn!"

After I said that prayer, I immediately went back to teaching and without even thinking of my hand I just went on with my day. My students needed me and my attention, and I was no longer sleepy! I never did get to drink a cup of coffee!

I taught the rest of the day and all through the Bible Club, and went home normally that night like nothing out of usual had happened that day! I literally forgot all about it. It was completely erased from my mind. I did not even tell my husband about it. It was as if it had never happened. My hand was completely normal, there was absolutely no sign whatsoever of any burn.

The next morning as usual, I got up early to go swimming before school, and I always take off my wedding ring and set it on top of the microwave until I get home. I just don't like to swim with it on in case something might happen to it in the pool.

My husband greeted me at the door after I came home from my swim, as he had noticed that my ring looked weird. He asked me, "What in the heck did you do yesterday that would cause your ring to look like this?"

I was embarrassed to tell him, but I did tell him what happened the day before, Both he and I were aware at that moment that a miracle had occurred. My ring was completely out of shape, it was no longer round. It had molded itself to the shape of my finger, and it was completely distorted and bent out of shape. It looked as if someone had taken the metal and just banged it hard to reshape it into a weird, distorted shape. It was completely deformed, but still intact. The diamond itself was the same.

I took the ring back to my favorite jeweler, the one who had heard the ring miracle number one.

Now I was back with the same ring and another miracle story. When I told him what happened this time, he said that the gold had melted to the shape of my finger and that could only have happened at an extremely high temperature, and that I should have been in the emergency room immediately after that happened. He testified that another miracle had happened to my ring, and that could be the only explanation in his professional experience.

Praise God! I should have been disfigured, but instead He supernaturally intervened and healed my hand!

Miracle #3: The jewelry box

This was a dream. I dreamed that I was in a glorious room that was filled from floor to ceiling with extravagantly decorated jewelry boxes. The entire room was so brilliant that your eyes could barely stand the reflection of the light! The boxes ranged in sizes, but all were completely covered in radiant diamonds! I felt as if I was in the jewelry storeroom of heaven!

I bent down to see one of the jewelry boxes and I realized that the boxes had tickets on them. One part of the ticket said "Admit One" and the other part had a name on it. I asked what the names meant, and the Lord told me that these were his children, his jewels.

I woke up realizing that some of those names were the names of students I had once taught!

The Lord, I feel, was telling me how happy he was with the Bishop Bible Club!

If you would like to read more miracle stories like this one, my former principal and friend Frances Purnell-Dampier, of Bishop Elementary School, published this and many other stories in her book, Miracles Blossom from the Spirit Within, published by Trafford Publishing in 2013.

Praying at Bishop

I used to walk down the hallways of Bishop in the mornings before school started, praying silently under my breath for the little kids that got there super early in the morning, obviously dropped off by some parents who had to get to work early. Sometimes I even asked them to help in in my classroom with something, just so that they could get in out of the cold and have someone to talk to. I would make stuff up for them to do like rearranging my books or setting out papers and pencils for me, just to give them a safe place to hide out.

Before the bell rang at 8:00AM, I would try to walk through the campus smiling at people and saying "Good Morning" to lots and lots of people, trying to give them a happy beginning to their day. Same thing, I would go out after school was over, and stand on my porch, and wave to people at they walked by, smiling and saying hi. I especially liked saying hi to all the little kids in strollers, or the little toddlers barely walking yet, stumbling along like little drunken soldiers! One day, a little kid came up to me and asked me if I was "the happy teacher"!

When we had an assembly, or a trip to art class, or to the library, I would make it a habit of praying as my line of straggling students tried to keep up with my fast clip of a pace, hoping that whoever was watching us would approve of their behavior. That needed a lot of praying!

So, it was not uncommon for me to pray during yard duty or recess breaks. Sometimes I would literally close the doors to my classroom and pray that the Holy Spirit would come in and bless my classroom that day! Especially on days when teaching was particularly challenging!

One day, I noticed a Special Education teacher friend of mine looking not the same. Her face looked drawn down and she appeared not to be herself! She has the biggest heart, and works with all the kids who have reading and learning disabilities. I immediately went up to her and took her hands and asked what was going on! She started to explain that out of the blue, no warning at all, she had come down with Bell's Palsy, a condition where parts of your face and body seem frozen and unable to move. The right side of her face was not able to smile, and when she spoke her face did not move normally along with her mouth.

Well, this was a time for prayer if I ever saw one! I asked if I could pray with her, and we did! Right in the middle of the playground, not caring who saw us, who listened, or who might inquire what was happening! We held hands I asked asked boldly for her to be healed of this in the name of Jesus, that His full and complete healing would come to her! By this time, some little kids had gathered around us and were listening! Who cares?

Then we had a vacation, like Christmas holiday, or some long vacation like that! After we all had returned after our break, I saw Mylene on the way back from the office at recess one day, and there she was looking completely normal and refreshed! I once again ran up to her and started holding her hands and rejoicing with her, yelling, "Mylene!! You look normal again! You're healed!! When we touched hands it was like a jolt of power went through the both of us! It felt like we had been hit with a spark! I know what that spark was! We felt it so strongly we started jumping up and down rejoicing and laughing and dancing about! People stopped and looked at us, and then just kept on their way! Probably thought we were a "bit touched"! She then told me that when I prayed with her, she shared it with her devout Catholic mom in the Philippines, and when her mom heard the story she immediately burst into tears and knew that Mylene was going to be healed! And she was! Praise God for answering her prayers and making her whole!

From then on, Mylene and I had a special friendship, and her aide and I got to be good friends too.

Shoe Troubles

My daughters and I wear the same size shoes, so when they would move away or get tired of a pair of shoes, I would think, "Oh Heck!, maybe I'll wear those some day!" So my shoe collection grew and grew exponentially with their frequent moves to college, and back, and to college again, and back, and so on!

I have shoes with wedge heels, shoes that are so high and tipsy I will never wear them, boots coming out of my ears, and jogging shoes for the next ten years! Then I have all my sensible teacher shoes, and glittery high heels for the cruises we used to take before COVID 19! And all the shoes I need for my messy pottery experiences, and gardening shoes, on and on!

Since I have so many, it is hard to know which ones to throw out first! They all range in ages from extremely old (I even have a pair of boots that my mother bought in bulk from Nordstrom in Seattle when I was in college in the 1970's, which actually are back in style now!) to rather current. But I've decided now that I am retired that I will never have to buy another pair of shoes again in my lifetime!

Three very funny stories happened with my shoes over the years. Remember when we were in Beijing visiting the temples and seeing the sights on the teacher's trip to China? Well, the day we visited the biggest temple in Beijing, while we were walking across the very bumpy and ancient stones, all of a sudden it felt like I was about to tip over! I was having a hard time balancing. I looked down and saw little chunks had come off the soles of my sandals! Literally, the half of the sole of my shoe had just crumpled off! I had to limp through the rest of that visit, trying to keep my balance the best I could, and when we finished we all had to take a detour to a shoe store so that I could get back to normal! Apparently, my shoes were so old that they just disintegrated!

A similar thing happened with my teacher friends again when I was taking a Line Dancing class through the City of Cupertino Recreation classes. A bunch of us teachers from Bishop decided it would be fun to take a class together. Mid way through the class we noticed these little chunks of rubber scattered all over the dance floor! Oh No! Now it was really embarrassing because some of the same teachers in the class were the ones that were with me in China! Same problem again, over aged shoes disintegrating!

It happened one more time, this time at work at Bishop. Just walking around during a normal school day, and the chunks flew off again! Oh geez!

Another problem with shoes was getting dressed so early in the morning that I couldn't distinguish between colors. I would get dressed in the dark when Nick was still asleep and race off to get to yoga at 6AM before school. I have been known to show up at school wearing one black shoe and one brown shoe, both sandals of the same style, but just different colors!

The last one happened at my yoga studio! One time I was in such a hurry to get out of there and off to school I took another lady's slip on clogs and left mine behind. When she came out of yoga class, her shoes were gone, and mine were left for her to wear! I had to show up at yoga the next day, with egg on my face, with the offending shoes in hand! Asking how do we find the owner, and may I please have my own shoes back?

Why am I thinking that I am sounding like Lucille Ball of I Love Lucy?

Ghost Night at Tulloch Castle

This memory is from my first trip to Scotland in the summer of the year 2017. We were traveling to a house share in Drum Oak, a suburb of Banchory and Aberdeen, with Jim and Sue, our relatives, and my husband Nick. We first flew into Manchester, England, where we picked up a manual transmission rental car, which both Jim and Nick were authorized to drive. Remember, in England and Scotland you drive on the left side of the street, so driving there can be quite the stressful situation until you get acclimatized to the changes. And since you are driving from the right side of the front of the car, the gear shift is all confusing and you have to shift with your left hand instead of the right! So difficult! Jim was the most experienced driver in Europe, so we let him take the lead and get us on our way!

We meandered our way through Northern England and Scotland, stopping at various bed and breakfasts, and eventually made it to

Drum Oak, Scotland. Here we were greeted by the friendly next door neighbors, who were gardening in their rather large organic garden in their side yard, who helped us unlock the key lock box to our three bedroom home for the next three weeks.

The house was in near proximity to a wonderful castle, which has a historic medieval tower and grand hall building, given to the Irvine family by Robert the Bruce in 1323. It is a statuesque landmark with beautiful rose gardens which have been cultivated since the 17th Century. We visited the historic Tearoom, ate buttery scones with strawberry jam, and drank English Breakfast tea, and looked over the surrounding forests which provide a home for red kites, roe deer, red squirrels, and badgers.

After a few days of touring Banchory and its surrounding Dee River, we headed off to do some more exploring in the Northern parts of Scotland. We eventually ended up in the city of Dingwall.

We had been driving all day, we finally arrived in the town and were truly exhausted. We made it to a rather down shodden hotel, on the outskirts of town. As we wearily just wanted to sit down, get a beer, and rest up for the night, we were informed by the hotel staff that we had only one reservation for that night. Apparently when we had made the reservations, one was for the night before, and we had already forfeited that room when we didn't show up. She reassured us that she would do her best to try to find other accommodations for us that night for one of the couples in our group.

Jim was feeling guilty as he had done all the reservations for all of us, so when she offered a rather pricey room in Tulloch Castle, one of fifteen haunted castles in Scotland, as our only other option, he and Sue gratefully took her up on her suggestion. Nick and I piled our suitcases into our crummy room, and we all drove up the magical hill to the castle, dropped Jim and Sue off, and made plans to meet up later than evening for dinner at the Castle.

We met up in the bar area, where the delightful and charmingly friendly bartender started entertaining us with stories about the Castle, and the ghosts who inhabited it, still to this day! As we drank our scotch and waters, he went on to tell us about how sometimes he would be working in the bar all by himself, and he could have sworn that he left a glass on one counter, only to turn around and find it mysteriously in a whole other place of the bar room! After twenty minutes of drinking our scotches, we were thoroughly ready to head off to the medieval dining room for a yummy meal, only to be pleasantly treated to a delightful dinner of traditional Scottish delights in the Turrets Restaurant. We enjoyed locally sourced dishes from an a la carte menu, accompanied by red wine of course! The bartender had invited us to join him later in the lobby for the Ghost Tour, which he would be leading after dinner.

Off we went on our Ghost Tour! This castle dates back to the 12th Century, and is known to be home to one of its resident ghosts, the Green Lady. She has been sighted so frequently in the bar area, that they actually named the bar after her! Over the years, a number of paranormal teams have investigated the castle, and have found some very interesting results. Orbs, balls of light, and icy cold patches of air have been seen and felt, and weird noises like clicks, bangs, and thuds have been recorded on film, with no explanation over the years.

At one point in the tour, he took us to the dungeon room, which was basically a huge hole in the ground, surrounded by a roped off chain link barricade. This is where hundreds of people were dropped in, to be left to suffer and starve to their deaths! No wonder there were so many ghosts lurking around this place!

He also explained that there was a whole labyrinth of secret tunnels underneath the house, where people could hide if they felt threatened by the villagers coming to attack them during Medieval wars.

On our tour, we encountered stone fireplaces, elaborately paneled rooms, original ceilings, and a massive family portrait where the Green Lady was so spooky that where ever you were in the room you felt her eyes traveling and following you.

Her father, Duncan Davidson, 4th Laird of Tulloch, was born in 1800, and went on to be locally known as "the Stag", having had five wives who bore his eighteen children, and he had at least thirty illegitimate children around the district! As the story goes, the bartender explained that one night he had been visiting the bedroom of one of his housemaids when his daughter discovered them in the arms of rapture! Later that night, the daughter mysteriously fell to her death down to the bottom of a staircase! Just how green she is, and the details of her existence we do not know, but she has been sighted over the centuries. A large portrait of her is displayed in the Grand Hall of the Castle.

During the tour, the bartender entertained us with stories of how certain rooms in the hotel have been known to be the Haunted rooms! He asked if any of us would be staying for the night, and to be aware if you felt someone trying to snuggle up in bed next to you, or if you felt fingers touching your shoulders in the night!

Nick and I gratefully dashed back to our car after dinner and the tour, back to our unhaunted crummy hotel room in the bad part of town, and said a prayer for Jim and Sue that they would survive the night! Which they did!! The next morning, as the sun was shining on the castle, all the spookiness seemed to disappear, and we were off once again on another adventure to another wonderful town!

Silly Times in Kenmore, Scotland

It was finally time to head up to the highlands of Perthshire, Scotland and check out the local sights. We ended up in a quaint, picturesque village of Kenmore, which is in the middle of mountains and surrounded by a lovely lake with boats and families on vacation, and a yummy bakery edging up to the lake.

As we checked into the Kenmore Hotel, immediately we were chuckling as we observed the help staff at the desk "smooze" with the customers about their accommodations. Just about every other call coming into the desk was registering some sort of complaint (mostly from American tourists, it seemed) ; no hot water, rickety steps, crummy internet, and the list went on and on. It was our home for one night, so we knew we would survive.

Yes, our rooms were a little on the small side, and when I went to take a bath, the water didn't flow out of the tap very well, and the room was decorated like my grannie's bedroom. It was then that we realized that this is the oldest hotel in all of Scotland! It was built first as a tavern in 1502, and the interior of the bar area and lobby still reflect that dated style. In the 17th Century, this hotel was where Cromwell's army dined. Queen Victoria and Prince Albert spent some of their honeymoon at this hotel! Her later impressive review of this part of Scotland greatly enhanced this area's popularity as a vacation spot. There were paintings of Robert "Robbie" Burns, a famous Scottish poet, in the bar area and one of his poems still remains on the chimney breast of the fireplace.

As we sat in the bar having a drink, we kept running into Scotsmen from the Orkney Islands and the Shetland Islands, who had brought their Labradoodles into the bar area with them. We were surrounded by dogs! And their dialects were so strong we could barely understand them!

We made our way to the dining room, which had a view of the Tay River, where outdoor dining was allowed. We dined indoors, and were continually entertained by the delightful help staff who were mostly from Spain, and Eastern Europe. Their dialects were also very hard to decipher, and there was general confusion about ordering, and the wine list, and as much as they tried to race around and help us, dinner was chaotic and still very pleasant. We kept joking that we felt like we were in the Faulty Towers Hotel, you know the BBC comedy television show!

As we were trying to check out the next morning, the hotel staff was being swamped and overwhelmed by hoards of tour bus travelers, who seemed to be mostly from the US, and used to all the creature comforts of home, which obviously were not possible in the hotel from the 1500's! At one point the maintenance guy was addressing one of the customer's requests, and finally just yelled out," I don't have that extra part, what do you want me to do, pull it out of my sphincter?" These were like usual New York City types, expecting everything to be first rate, and unwilling to accept that this hotel was what it was, not going to be what you might want or expect!! At this point, we were almost in hysterics!! Trying to the best of our abilities to muffle our laughter, and just rolling our eyes at what we were observing. The maintenance guy ended up running out of the hotel, so exasperated, and took off across the street, and just left the work and the lobby behind!

After this, we meandered down to the lake front, and went into a charming bakery, who had a baker with a real attitude. Jim went up to the counter to order his tea and crumpets, and she greeted him with a grouchy scowl, and demanded " What do you want?" Jim came back with a great big smile and said, "Gee, can't you sweeten up a little there, honey?" She immediately cracked up laughing like crazy, and the whole atmosphere in the bakery changed. Obviously, the workers in this town were frequently overwhelmed by fussy, over the top tourists. We did our best to appreciate all their hard work, and delightful services, and went on our way to the next marvelous adventure! I highly recommend visiting this charming town if you ever get the chance!

Balancing Act

I wrote this on August 1, 2003 I don't know why I wrote it, or for what occasion. Maybe just musing and thinking about my life.

Being a mom is like learning to walk.

Knowing when to stand up for what you know to be right, and when to keep it to yourself.

It's learning to put everyone else before yourself when necessary

And when to finally think of yourself.

When to let your children be free enough to make some mistakes

And then strong enough within yourself to accept who they have become

If I've learned anything from all the balancing I've done

It's never to forget who you fell in love with first

Never lose sight of the love you have with your most precious one -

Your husband

Your soulmate

Your life.

Yummy Polenta, a Gin and Tonic, and a Cherry Pie

During the year of 2020 I have been participating in helping pack bags of water, granola bars, crackers, fruit, sandwiches, desserts, and breads for 105 low-income or homeless families with my church members at West Valley Presbyterian Church. We also serve a freshly made hot meal, which was cooked that day in our church kitchen, and then wrapped up in an individual to go container. We pick up donated desserts from the Safeway Church in Sunnyvale, CA. on Saturday morning, and then cut them up into serving sizes and put them in styrofoam containers too. We do this on the last Saturday of each month. This month the day occurred on Halloween, October 31st!

As usual, my husband and I made fifty peanut butter and jelly sandwiches in our kitchen on Saturday morning. We've been doing that for months. Then I set off to help pack the bags with my other fifteen or so friends in McHattie Hall. The couple who ordinarily cooks and packages the hot meal was taking a vacation from cooking, so a five star gourmet team of chefs from two local restaurants were cooking three huge pots yummy, mascarpone cheese creamy polenta, chubby braised Italian sausages, olive oil and garlic simmered sliced red peppers, sauteed onions, and spears of broccolini. The kitchen smelled heavenly like an Italian grandmother's kitchen! They finished up cooking the meal, transferred the food into oven sized warming pans, and left the kitchen to go off to their real jobs that Saturday night!

We finished up getting all the bags of non perishable foods packing into all 105 brown paper bags, and loaded them up into two large vans to be taken to the Murphy Park drop off point.

Then came the job of dishing up the 105 styrofoam divided trays of the yummy Italian feast! We worked in an assembly line, one huge scoop of polenta in the tray first, another person giving two large braised sausages, I was in charge of spooning in a large scoop of red peppers and onions, and the broccolini went on the top. Another person sealed up the tray, and stacked them in boxes to go into the vans.

After completing that task, we were once again loading all these trays up into more vans for transport to the park. As you can imagine, it took a huge amount of team effort to complete that task! We had so much food left over, we dug through the kitchen cabinets and found some to go Tupperware containers so that all the workers who desired to could take some home for a Saturday night feast! Still, we had lots of polenta left over! I didn't want it to go to waste, so I started loading up the yummy polenta in the remaining styrofoam containers, and I must have made seven more. And still we had leftovers! They must have made enough polenta for 160 people!

Now, it was about 4:30 in the afternoon, and the lines of people awaiting these yummy delights were starting to line up at the park awaiting the drop offs. I stayed behind with one other friend to clean up the kitchen, wash all the dirty pans and utensils, and reorganize them into their perspective drawers and cabinets in the kitchen. I was so focused on completing the task of washing all the dishes, and rising them, and putting them on the drying rack I was just looking ahead and working furiously away! I finished up all the pans that were loaded into the sink, only to turn around to find that I had another 15 or so big sticky pans to clean, coated with goopy yellow polenta, oily pans of red pepper juices, buttery onion pans, and more browned bits of sausages on aluminum warming pans from the oven, and three huge baking sheets covered with the remains of the broccolini!

The work seemed like it was never going to end! I worked so furiously sometimes the water for rinsing would shoot up into my face, and cover me with a blast! Eventually, we got the kitchen looking like a professional cleaning crew had been there, and I loaded up the dirty aprons and hot pads into my car, along with several styrofoam trays filled with the yummy leftovers. I finally was free!

Now it was about 6 PM and as I was driving home, I was thinking about what I could possibly do with all that polenta! I walked in the door, and Nick could see by the look on my face that I was clearly exhausted, and the first thing he asked was "Can I fix you a drink?", which, of course, I said, "Yes", and I proceeded to run myself a wonderfully hot bubble bath. I sipped on my Gin and tonic while luxuriating in my hot steamy water! Such heaven!

As soon as I sat down at the kitchen counter to visit with my husband while we warmed up our Italian leftovers, I told Nick that we should take two containers of polenta to our next door and across the street neighbors.

I have a habit of giving random gifts to my neighbors, like if I have too many plums on the fruit trees, I will just leave random bags of fruit on my neighbors' doorsteps. Or, if I have too much arugula in the garden, I know one particular neighbor who adores it, and I just ring the doorbell and leave it there. Or, if I see a neighbor, even someone I don't really know, but I recognize them from walking past day after day, I will holler out from my garden and ask them if they would like a bunch of fresh basil, some broccoli, or some Swiss chard! I just grab the plant out of the dirt, shake it off a bit, run into the house to get a plastic bag, and run out the door to give it to them! Whatever I have too much of, I give away to neighbors, friends, or donate.

Since this night was no exception, and I had already changed into my jammies for the night, I urged Nick to do the delivering for me this time! He begrudgingly left with two containers of polenta in his hands, and rang the next door neighbor's doorbell, with no response, so just as he was giving up, the neighbor's wife showed up in the driveway, just returning from an errand! He gave her the styrofoam container, and she thanked him profusely, and he came back to deliver the other. These types of coincidences happen all the time to us when I try to do good deeds in our neighborhood! I texted my other neighbor, he said eh would drop by in five minutes to get the polenta. He showed up with a huge slice of crunchy topped cherry pie, my favorite!

Last Christmas, I made homemade embroidered tote bags, embroidered felt Christmas stockings, home made plum jam, home baked cranberry orange loaf breads, and little dishes of pottery that I had glazed, and wrapped them up in bags with bows and delivered them to my neighbors. Sometimes I would ring the door bell, and leave disappointed, only to have the neighbor come up the driveway at that instant coming home from a walk or an errand. Other times, I will race out the door to give something to someone, and they will have just driven up!

These "coincidences" happen to me all the time! Say what you will, and think what you want, be I prefer to think that these are little nudges from the Holy Spirit encouraging me to continue to be generous to my neighbors and even strangers.

The other day, a sweet new family with little kids moved into the neighborhood and I had made two large loaves of pumpkin bread thinking that they might appreciate a friendly gesture. Then I remembered that we are living in COVID 19 times, and they might not appreciate a baked good from a stranger, so instead I drooped a hand made tote bag on their front door handle, and a little note welcoming them to the neighborhood! I have never met these people, but I am hoping that some day, when all this social distancing is finally over, we will finally meet at a neighborhood event, and we can really introduce ourselves to each other.

So, as you can see, it wasn't a typical Halloween, no trick or treaters, no costumes to wear, no Jack o Lanterns were carved, but we still had a wild, active day of fun! And I still went to bed exhausted. I think I slept in until 9AM the next day, which for me is a hugely rare event!

Wrapping It Up!

As you probably have noticed, most of my experiences molded me and made me into the person I am today. I truly believe that each one of us can have a significant impact on the ones we love, and our world. Our actions don't have to be spectacular by any means, just simple acts of showing that we see someone for where they are.

Being true to me has always meant showing my care and concern for others in acts of service and kindness. This probably stems from my early childhood experiences of being self-reliant and independent. In my way of thinking, I've always been the "doer" or the one who got started on a project and just finished it, without much fretting or thought about it. My family would call that my "campin" style" of living.... don't worry too much about the small stuff, just do your best. Whether it is knitting a hat for someone, or giving somebody some salad greens from my garden, or making some banana bread, and tucking it into one of my handmade bowls, I'm just a person who has always had her hands busy doing something for someone. And tons of prayers going up as I'm thinking of those I serve.

So, as you have read these stories, I hope you have seen some of yourself in some of them, and have thought that maybe you shouldn't take life so seriously. Go on that trip without an agenda, free as the wind, and see what you find out about the world! Figure out a way to be less dependent on store bought goods, and learn a new skill that you can teach others!

I've always said that if the world goes bonkers, and we all have to do things differently, I'll be the first in line to share my skills and talents with others. I could teach you how to make your own bread, sew your own quilts, knit your own hats and socks, can your own jam, plant and harvest your own food, dry your own herbs, make your own dinners, prune your own fruit trees, make your own cups and bowls, weave your own bags, embroider your own clothes, and follow your own path! Ask God to direct your paths, and listen to that small voice. Then ponder how you can follow what you know to be right and honorable and true.

Actually, I actually had a principal at Bishop Elementary who understood that about me. If I was knitting during a staff meeting or district training, I paid better attention if my hands were busy! He let me bring my knitting wherever I went, as long as I wasn't busy passing notes or smirking under my breath and making my peers distracted along with me! So, sometimes in your life, hopefully you will be blessed with bosses who will understand your quirks and let you be you! I had quite a few of those in all my years of working!

I truly hope you have found some light hearted humor on these pages, and that these stories have encouraged you to follow your own unique journey to find your inner freedom! At least, those of you who know me well, will now better understand what makes "Kale Mary" the unique person I am!

Thanks to all my friends and family who have encouraged me in my path to find God and peace, and acceptance of all my shortcomings! But most of all, don't take life too seriously, and get out

and try something new!

Made in the USA
Coppell, TX
19 December 2020